Education Under Occupation

TRANSGRESSIONS: CULTURAL STUDIES AND EDUCATION
Volume 12

In this book, the author critically analyzes the ongoing and wide-ranging effects of colonialism and globalization on the poor, especially on those living in the "Third World." The author's overarching argument is that colonization was not merely about the conquest of foreign lands, but it was also about the ideological monitoring of the colonized's mind, often maintained through western hegemonic texts and institutional apparatus, such as schools and churches. Analyzing and situating colonialism in the context of western neo-liberal policy of occupation and economic, political, and ideological dominations, the author thus demonstrates how, through schools and the mass corporate media, neocolonized and occupied subjects have been mis-educated to internalize and reproduce old western values, beliefs, and norms at the expense of their own.

Pierre W. Orelus, a former high school teacher, is currently a doctoral candidate at the University of Massachusetts-Amherst and teaches at Cambridge College and Holyoke Community College. His research interest includes critical literacy, postcolonial studies, and pedagogy for self-liberation and liberation of others. Pierre has spoken nationally and internationally on these issues.

Through his recent academic work, Pierre has been exploring the intersection between language, culture, and literacy, and the role these concepts play in the construction of human subjectivity and vision of the world.

Education Under Occupation
The Heavy Price of Living in a Neocolonized and Globalized World

Pierre W. Orelus
University of Massachusetts-Amherst, MA, USA

SENSE PUBLISHERS
ROTTERDAM / TAIPEI

A C.I.P. record for this book is available from the Library of Congress.

ISBN: 978-90-8790-145-5 (paperback)
ISBN: 978-90-8790-146-2 (hardback)
ISBN: 978-90-8790-147-9 (ebook)

Published by: Sense Publishers,
P.O. Box 21858, 3001 AW Rotterdam,
The Netherlands

Printed on acid-free paper

Cover image: Photograph of mural courtesy of Kamil Peters, © Kamil Peters.

I want to dedicate this book to my proud mama, Leanne "Daya" Adelson. I cannot ever thank her enough for her pure love, for sacrificing her own education so that I could have one, and for raising me and my three other siblings with almost no support from my dad. My mama did not read to me "bed time stories" because she simply did not know how, and also because she was too busy struggling daily to feed and cloth me. However, she made time to teach me three vital things: respect myself and others, take pride in myself, and place my human dignity above all. She is my real role model and shero.

TABLE OF CONTENTS

PREFACE/ACKNOWLEDGEMENTS

Although this book was already conceptualized for more than a decade, I embarked on the journey of writing it in 2004, a year after I started a doctoral program at the University of Massachusetts at Amherst. My plan was to finish writing it in the summer of 2005. However, the daily struggle of survival as a doctoral student, i.e., holding part time teaching and research assistant jobs at different institutions to support myself and family members did not allow me to do so. In the summer 2006, while I was in the midst of finishing the book manuscript, my wife and I lost our first baby as a result of a miscarriage. Three years before I started writing this book, three airplanes destroyed the world trade center in New York. Such a tragic event cost thousands of innocent lives. In 2002, the Unites States (U.S.) attacked Afghanistan and overthrew the Talibans, who were accused of providing a safe heaven to Osama Bin laden. The following year the U.S. and Great Britain and allies invaded Iraq and overthrew Sadam Hussein under the pretext that Sadam had nuclear weapons and therefore was a danger to the world. Since the U.S. invasion and occupation of these two countries, thousands of people including children and elderly have been killed. Recently, in July 2006 Israel and Ezbollah, a military re-sistant Lebanese group, were involved in a war that cost the life of thousands of innocent people in Lebanon and in Israel, particularly in Lebanon. This is to point out that this book was written during very challenging personal and political mo-ments, which greatly influenced my thought while I was writing it.

This book critically analyzes and presents complex ideas in a very accessible way to readers, especially to novices who might not be familiar with colonial, neo-colonial, and "postcolonial" theories. It does so by defining unfamiliar terms and using those terms in very specific socioeconomic, educational, cultural, political, and economic contexts. Furthermore, this book does not only use those terms to talk about the harmful effects of western neocolonial and neoliberal policies on "Third World" countries–it clearly proposes alternative ways to counter western hegemonic cultural, political, and economic influences on these countries.

This book is very timely and necessary in that it will greatly contribute to colonial, neocolonial, and postcolonial discourses, particularly in the diaspora. Given its clarity and accessibility in analyzing a complex set of ideas around issues of west-ern hegemony and resistance of the subaltern to the western neocolonial power, this book will occupy a distinctive place in the realm of academy and beyond. It will certainly attract and be relevant to the needs of undergraduate, graduate stu-dents, and scholars in the fields of teacher education, neocolonial and "postcolo-nial" studies, history, political science, sociology, and economics. This book will also be beneficial to general readers interested in reading personal narratives about the impact of western neocolonial and neoliberal policies on neocolonized coun-tries.

This book, like anything else in life that I thus far have managed to accomplish, could not have been made possible without the love, support of my family, friends, colleagues, and mentorship of some professors. I would like to show my gratefulness to my partner, la reina de la casa, Romina Pacheco-Orelus whose love and undying support have given the strength to finish the manuscript of this book despite lonely and difficult moments. I want to express my endless gratitude to Professor Joe Kincheloe not only for his mentorship, genuine support, and intellectual inspiration, but also for the trust he invested in me by allowing me to publish my first book through his book series. Many thanks also go to the folks at Sense Publishers, Michel Lokhorst and Peter de Liefde, whose hard work made the materialization of this book possible. I am immensely grateful to Professors Noam Chomsky, Sonia Nieto, and Pepi Leisyna for their insightful comments on the book prospectus, several chapters of the book manuscript, and for their mentorship and intellectual inspiration. To similar degree as Professor Joe Kincheloe, Professors Chomsky, Nieto, and Leistyna's, constructive feedback helped me strengthen my arguments throughout the book. Of course, I should be only held responsible for any claim that I made and any position that I took in the book. I owe a deep debt to my undergraduate Professor Ann Withorn for her continued mentorship and genuine support. My sincere gratitude also goes to Professors Cesar A. Rossatto, Enoch Page, Agustin Lao, Sangeeta Kama, and Josna Rege for their valuable support and intellectual inspiration. Many thanks go to my academic advisor, Jerri Willett, and Professors Magaret Gehbard, Pat Paugh, and Theresa Austin for their invaluable support. I am very grateful to my friends and classmates Jean Grimard Blaise, Lumumba Shabaka, Estephen Noel, Margaret Boyko, Yasser Muniff, Elsa Wiehe, Gloria Barragan, Milton Joshua, Kathy Mcdonough, Jane Carey, and my brother in law, Rafael Pacheco, for their support and strong encouragement during the conceptualization of this book. I wish to thank Professor Marsha Rudman, my friends Rachel Briggs, Nicole Calandra, Erold Bailey, Gardy Guiteau, Simon Safouda, and Frank Johnson for their feedback on the book manuscript and the book proposal. I would like to express my sincere thankfulness to my high school mentor, Paul Ascencio, and history high school teacher, Jean Reynold Jean Pierre, whose early mentorship and inspiration helped me widen my knowledge and shaped my political and critical consciousness. I am sincerely grateful to Kamil Peters, a local artist living in western Massachusetts, and the group of talented boys and girls he has been working with, for allowing me to use the mural they designed and drew on the cover of my book. I am also immeasurably appreciative to Frantz Fanon, Antenor Firmin, Jacques Roumain, Charlemagne Peralte, Jacques Stephen Alexis, Toussaint Louverture, Gayatri Chakravorty Spivak, Edwidge Danticat, Vandana Shiva, Maryse Conde, Amical Cabral, Paulo Freire, Walter Rodney, C.L.R. James, Edward Said, Antonio Gramsci, Malcom X, Albert Memmi, Ngugi wa Thongo, Chandra Mohanty, Andre Lord, bell hooks, Patrice Lumumba, Thomas Sankara, Arundhati Roy, Henry Giroux, Ernesto "Che" Guevara, Winnie and Nelson Mandela, Howard Zin, Peter McClaren, Donaldo Macedo, Aime Cesaire, Amy Goodman, and Cornel West whose scholarly work, heroism, unshakable political conviction, and ideological position have challenged me to critically reflect on, actively engage with and act on the world. Finally, but not least, I want to sincerely thank other members of my family, namely my brother, Lionel Orelus, his wife and two children, Carline Orelus, Jeffery and Jennifer Orelus, and my sister Freda Orelus for their love and endless support.

INTRODUCTION

Interrogating The Western World-Towards a Better Understanding of The Restern World: A Historical Inventory

As the true radicals of postcolonial theory will tell you, we are hardly in a "postcolonial" moment. The official apparatus might have been removed, but the political, economic, and cultural links established by colonial domination still remain with some alterations.

Robin Kelly, In Aime Cesaire, *Discourse on Colonialism.*

Many of the post-colonial writers bear their past within them-as scars of humiliating wounds, as instigation for different practices, as potentially revised visions of the past tending towards a future, as urgently re-interpretable and re-deployable experiences in which the formerly silent native speaks and acts on territory taken back from the colonialist. And, for the first time, these writers can read the great colonials masterpieces that had not only misrepresented them, but had assumed their inability to read and respond directly to what had been written about them, just as European ethnography depended in very real measure upon the natives' incapacity to intervene in scientific discourse about them. Let us try now to review the new situations more fully

Edward Said, Intellectuals in the Post-Colonial World

INTRODUCTION

For many of us "postcolonial" subjects colonization is not over. We continue to be surrounded by and subjected to colonial practices via many public and private institutions, such as schools, churches, families, workplaces, and the mass media. Hence, synthesizing both what Robin Kelly and Edward Said mentioned above, I would argue that colonization has merely taken a different ideological, economic, and political form as the history of the world has changed in the last fifty years or so. Even when some of us are now able to deconstruct lies embedded in colonial masterpieces about our identity, culture, and history, we still continue facing the challenge to fight for an accurate representation of ourselves through texts. My contention is that the material disaster that came along with colonization is not as profound as the psychological scar it has caused "postcolonial" subjects. The legacy of western politics of coloniality, i.e., forcible ownership of the colonized's territorial space paired up with an ideological running machine put in place to control their mind, has been carried over in the neocolonial and neoliberal era, and it is pervasive. To be precise, the ongoing western politics of cultural and historical misrepresentation of "postcolonial" subjects might be subtle, but it continues to cause damages to our subjectivity and sense of self. As Dei (2006) observes:

> Colonialism, read as imposition and domination, did not end with the return of political sovereignty to colonized peoples or nation states. Colonialism is not dead. Indeed, colonialism and re-colonizing projects today manifest themselves in variegated ways, e.g. the different ways knowledges get reproduced and receive validation within schools, the particular experiences of students that get counted as invalid and the identities that receive recognition and response from school authorities. (p. 2).

Thus, to counter the continuously ruinous effect of the legacy of colonialism, it is imperative that neocolonial subjects develop an anti- neocolonial discourse to critically interrogate and contextually situate historical and political events that have shaped their neocolonial lived experience. Further, they ought to use such a discourse to critically analyze and question the neocolonial social, cultural, educational, and political milieu that impacts them, rather than being passive spectators of this milieu.

Education under Occupation; The Heavy Price of Living in a Neocolonized and Globalized World, as a critical anti-colonial project, is situated at the crossroad of western neocolonial and neoliberal agenda to offer alternative ways of resisting such an agenda. With this said, this book critically analyzes the legacy of colonialism alongside the impact of western neocolonial and neoliberal policies on neocolonized countries. It maps out the colonial encounter and its aftermath. It does so by shifting from a longstanding influential Eurocentric way of thinking and method of analysis and seeking other analytical and ideological lenses to unveil and analyze the deep-seated educational, economic, political, and cultural wounds colonialism left as legacy.

Traditionally, studies on colonialism have focused on the dichotomy and asymmetrical power relations between the colonizer and the colonized. These studies have often looked at the colonized as a subordinate subject and the colonizer as a dominating subject. However, for the last two decades or so, other studies, such as "postcolonial" studies, have gone beyond the binary opposing the colonizer to the colonized to suggest optional ways to explore cultural, political, historical, and economic effects that the legacy of colonialism has engendered. These studies have also examined the extent to which colonial and now "postcolonial" subjects have used their human agency to challenge and resist such a legacy. "Postcolonial" theorist Ngugi wa Thongo (1965), in his seminal work *Decolonizing the Mind (1965))*, has looked at how colonialism has impacted the mind and identities of "postcolonial" subjects. Ngugi has also demonstrated the important role of one's human agency in the struggle against colonialism and its aftermath.

Partially drawing on colonial and "postcolonial" theorists' theoretical framework (e.g. Fanon, 1963; Memmi, 1969; Ngugi wa Thiongo, 1965; Cabral, 1970; Said, 1978; Nkrumah, 1970; Young, 2001; and Bhabha, 1983,1994, among others), I critically look at the ongoing and wide-ranging effects of colonialism from multiple angles. I first demonstrate how educationally, culturally, politically, and economically the legacy of colonialism has impacted neocolonized subjects, particularly women in restern countries. By restern countries, I mean countries in the Americas (except Canada and the United States), in Africa, in Asia, in the Caribbean, in Eastern Europe, and in the Middle East that have been economically and politically dominated and exploited and culturally influenced and, worse, alienated by western imperial powers, such as the United States, Great Britain, and France. I go on to delineate how western neocolonial and neoliberal policies have engendered the displacement and migration of neocolonized subjects from their native lands to western lands. Specifically, I show the correlation between western neocolonial and neoliberal policies against neocolonized countries and the massive migration of neocolonized subjects to imperial lands, such as the United States, Spain, France, and Great Britain.

My central argument is that colonization was not only about the conquest of foreign lands. Equally catastrophic, colonization was about the ideological monitoring of the colonized's mind often maintained through western hegemonic texts and institutional apparatus, such as schools and churches. Thus, throughout the book I demonstrate how through schools neocolonized subjects have been miseducated to internalize and reproduce old western values, beliefs, and norms at the expense of their own.

To contextually locate the everlasting influence and negative effects of colonialism on colonial and neocolonial subjects, I use neocolonialism as one of the major themes throughout the book to analyze the unequal economic and political power dynamics between the West and the Rest. Here, the Rest is defined and referred to as colonized, neocolonized, invaded, and occupied countries, which one generally names as the "Third World." With regard to the western neoliberal economic and political agenda, issues such as globalization, are explored to analytically explicate western exploitations of neocolonized countries. Inhuman working conditions of Haitian and Indian farmers and factory workers are used as a case in point to demonstrate how this has been orchestrated by the International Monetary Fund (IMF), the World Trade Organization (WTO), and the World Bank (WB).

Using a personal narrative as a "postcolonial" subject, I offer an insider perspective of the political and economic devastations of Haiti caused by neoliberal economic and political policies of western imperial powers, including the United States. I position myself as an insider to talk about the negative effects of western economic and political policies on Haiti, for too often many outsiders have claimed to understand the other's struggles and experiences. I believe that the time now comes for the "subaltern" (Spivak, 1988) to firmly stand and speak in their authentic voice about their own lived experience. The invader, the occupier, in short the oppressor has only throughout history spoken falsely in behalf of the subaltern. How could it have been otherwise? Has not that been the ever-present agenda of western colonialists?

As laid out below in the chapter outline, I address in this book issues related to western economic and political exploitations of formerly colonized countries, such as Haiti and India. I am fully aware that my critical analysis of these issues might upset or anger privileged groups of people who want to maintain the status quo. If that is the case, I will certainly understand their anger or denial, for "truth" coming from the oppressed sometimes hurts the feelings of privileged groups and threatens their economic and political interests. However, I am hoping that they will be angry with themselves and more importantly attempt to find the source of their anger, which might be grounded in and motivated by their economic greed and their social and political positions in an "uneven world" (Radhakrishnan, 2003). If this happens, I will be happy for this might be a good sign of their awareness and consciousness of their racial, social class, and corporate privileges. If, after expressing their guilt for accumulating so much privilege at the expense of others, they are willing to take action against their own privilege for a fair and equitable world, I will be even happier. This is part of what I am hoping for in writing this book. This might sound like a utopia in a world where the powerful through exploitation and extreme greed are silently killing the powerless. By the powerful, I mean CEOS of corporate organizations, such as the World Bank, the International Monetary Fund, the World Trade Organization, and other dominant groups of people in both the western and restern world that have exploited poor people in the Caribbean, Latin America, Asia, Africa, and in some Eastern European countries.

As demonstrated throughout the book, the unequal power relations between the West and the Rest remain a human tragedy. However, this tragedy ironically has not been at the center of western world forums that have focused on "human issues". Multiple summits organized by western imperial powers to address these issues have simply been a deception to the poor living in restern countries. The more western powerful countries talk about poverty in restern countries, the more things stay the same. In my opinion, all these world summits organized by western empires to talk about the rampant poverty that has economically, politically, and socially destabilized restern countries have been thus far merely a confession of guilt without any concrete action to follow it. The goal of the West is and has always been to ensure that the West remains powerful and independent and the Rest stays powerless and dependent. The West does not seem to have any interest in joining the Rest at the economic and political rendezvous where the wealth of the world, which it has confiscated for centuries, should be equally distributed.

In *Orientalism*, the late Said (1978) unravels the unequal power relations between the West and the "other." Said demonstrates how historically the western world has managed to maintain this uneven power relation by denigrating the Orientals through symbolic images that misrepresent them. The West has used these symbolic images, which portray the Orientals as simply exotic, passive, obedient, and, worse yet, as savage creatures, to politically and economically dominate the oriental world. Said puts it in these terms: "There are Westerners, and there are Orientals. The former dominate; the latter must be dominated, which usually means having their land occupied, their internal affairs rigidly controlled, their blood and treasure put at the disposal of one or another Western power" (p.36). Although in this study Said focused primarily on the asymmetrical power dynamics between Occidentals and Orientals, his argument is quite relevant to many issues that I addressed in this book. They range from restern countries' political and economic dominations by western neocolonial powers to cultural alienation and misrepresentation of neocolonial subjects.

As western imperial powers have shifted their economic and political policies from colonialism to neocolonialism, it is imperative that we, neocolonial subjects and allies, stay ideologically and politically alert so we can map out such a gigantic shift and resist it. Resisting this shift will require us to seek a new political and ideological terrain that enables us to shape what is happening both locally and globally, as the local informs the global and vice versa. Given that the local and the global are intertwined, one can no longer analyze what happens on a local level without linking it to what happens globally. Humanist and activist intellectuals, such as Noam Chomsky, Howard Zin, Joe Kincheloe, Edward Said, Arundhati Roy, Frantz Fanon, Jean Paul Sartre, Antonio Gramsci, and Peter McLaren, among others, have demonstrated through their work they understand the importance of such a link. This is what makes their humanist, activist, and scholarly work humanly stimulating and inspiring to many of us who have been standing firmly against western neocolonialism and neoliberalism.

As countries that were colonized have been experiencing a new form of colonization, neocolonial subjects, including the masses, those in the academia, and allies, have an obligation to stay politically engaged with the world and act upon it. By that I mean they ought to take part in any grassroots movement aiming to fight against the western neocolonial and neoliberal agenda, an agenda that is intended to exploit and dehumanize farmers and factory workers, especially female factory workers, in the restern world. The struggle against the western neocolonial and neoliberal agenda is a human struggle that every concerned citizen, who is fighting for social and economic justice, should be engaged in. In other words, this is not a struggle that only concerns or should only concern marginalized neocolonial subjects, such as poor farmers and factory workers in Haiti, India, and Afghanistan, but it should also concern us all.

Furthermore, to rigorously and effectively counter the western neocolonial and neoliberal agenda, more social political forums, like the ones that took place in Brazil in 2005, in Venezuela in 2006, and in Kenya this year are necessary. At these forums, political space was created for the masses to actively be a part of the debate on issues, such as globalization, unjust war, unjustified invasion and occupation of restern countries' territories, and the objectification of human beings living there. The reason for the masses' active participation in the debate revolved around these issues is that they are often the main victims of these corporate actions motivated by the political and economic greed of western imperial powers.

To de-imperialize the world, more social forums, such as those mentioned above, are needed. In addition, we need an anti-colonial framework to guide us in our communal movements to reclaim our stolen inalienable educational and human rights. These rights were taken away from us since the colonizer invaded our space and built a colonial-based educational, political, and legal system which, even decades after they were forced to "leave," has continuously served their interest. Given this historical fact, the collective struggle to salvage our identities and humanity would require a historical consciousness. Such a consciousness combined with our cultural resources and spiritual strength would empower us to identify and act upon colonial legacies that continue to psychologically, economically, and politically impact us to this day.

It must be made clear here that despite the ambitious aim of this book in terms of how it tackles and analyzes pressing colonial and neocolonial issues, it does not presume to hold all the solutions to the myriad problems that neocolonized subjects have been facing in this age of western neocolonial and neoliberal world. It is written in the hope that it will be served as entry points into debates and dialogues aimed to confront and dismantle neoliberal and neocolonial practices that continue to sub-humanize both westerners and resterners. Thus, I hope the content of this book will be served as an ideological inspiration to those who have already engaged in these debates and dialogues, as well as to those who are about to engage in them.

What this anti-colonial project could not offer, in terms of how to go about strategically to take to pieces the neocolonial and neoliberal machine, will be the gigantic task of future generations to take on. The reason is that the fight against the ubiquitous harmful effects of colonialism and neocolonialism on the "other" will be a lifetime long struggle, however sad and depressing this might sound. Therefore, it will be dishonest and pretentious on my part to claim that the content of this book is a panacea to countless problems that both resterners and westerners have been facing in this unjust world.

CHAPTER OUTLINE

Using a personal narrative, I begin the first chapter, "Imagine the Life of the Neocolonized in the Restern World," by providing a thorough analysis of how the legacy of colonialism continues to impact the culture, the educational, economic, and political systems of formerly colonized countries, such as Haiti. I argue that in school, most Haitian students are assimilated into the colonizer's language, French, at the expense of their native tongue, Creole. Later in the chapter, I explore how the western economic and political policies towards Haiti have particularly impacted poor Haitian farmers. Like farmers in other restern countries, the majority of Haitian farmers are forced to abandon their farms where they used to grow crops to feed themselves and their families. I argue that these farmers have abandoned their farms because they have not been able to compete with western technological advances and the overwhelming importation of products from the West. I conclude the chapter by pointing out how, like most restern countries, Haiti has been economically exploited and politically squeezed by the West.

Chapter two, "The Restern World: From Western Colonial to Western Neocolonial Domination," provides a brief theoretical review of colonialism, setting the tone to explore how the U.S. has executed its neocolonial agenda in neocolonized countries through the use of the International Monetary Fund, the World Bank, and the World Trade Organization. I argue that the U.S. uses these monstrous corporate organizations and corrupt leaders of neocolonized countries to strengthen and expand its economic and political power. However, nationalist leaders, who have opposed U.S. political and economic orders and policies, have been overthrown, put in jail, or simply killed. I situate my analysis of these huge corporations in the context of the United States' overall neocolonial and neoliberal agenda, which aims to divide and conquer. That is, a political and economic agenda intended to create a climate of political and economic terror in restern countries so it can justify its invasion and occupation of these countries.

Chapter three, "Noam Chomsky and Pierre Orelus: A Dialogue about the Impact of Colonialism and Imperialism on Restern Countries," starts off with an in-depth analysis of the history of British colonialism in India. This chapter explores the negative effects of British colonial power on India. It goes on to make evident the connection between western neocolonialism and corporate organizations, such as the World Bank and the World Trade Organization, and how these organizations have impoverished countries, such as India, Haiti, and Nicaragua, among others. Multiple political and economic aspects of United States' and Great Britain's globalization agenda are examined in the chapter. For example, the slaughtering of the Haitian pigs in the 80's by the Haitian government, due to the manipulation and complicity of the U.S. government, is used as a case in point to illustrate how the U.S. economic globalization agenda operates in neocolonized lands.

Chapter four, "Education under Occupation," maps out western occupation of restern countries and how it has tremendously impacted the school system of these countries. I begin this chapter by defining the term occupation and then analytically providing a historical account of it. While I do point out the socio-economic, cultural, political, and environmental effects of western occupation on occupied people, I mainly focus on the extent to which the learning of students living in the restern world has been negatively impacted by western occupation of their lands. Based on my understanding of what a dialogical learning and teaching relationship between teachers and students should look like in practice, I go on to lay out what a progressive philosophy of education should entail. Then, I examine the complexity of the teaching task of progressive teachers who have been teaching under occupation and explore, at the same time, the role that servant teachers of the occupying forces play in maintaining the status quo. I argue that, while progressive teachers help students develop political consciousness and critical thinking skills to challenge the status quo and effect social change, reactionary teachers mis-educate students by ideologically programming their mind to work for and serve the corporate interests of the occupying force and the dominant class in society.

In chapter five, "De-westernize World History," I interrogate the western hegemonic version of world history. Specifically, I analyze how the voices of restern heroic people have been silenced and placed in a narrow western historical box. This has resulted from the hegemonic version of world history by western imperial powers. Thus, I argue that world history should acknowledge and incorporate in history textbooks the great contribution of non-western historical figures, such as Toussaint Louverture and Simon Bolivar, who also shaped the history of the world. Finally, I analytically demonstrate how the dominant class has been trying to control the past by concealing historical facts from neocolonial subjects.

Chapter six, "The Subaltern Language under Western Siege," demonstrates how, through the history of colonialism, slavery, and western neoliberal and neo-colonial educational policies, languages other than English, French, and Spanish (not from Spain) have been subjugated. It goes on to demonstrate how this linguistic assault against indigenous languages and dialects has been perpetuated in schools through the teaching practices of teachers who often teach with a neocolonized and neoliberal mind. This chapter makes an appeal to decolonize the school system and the mind of the school personnel who is often in complicity with these neocolonial and neoliberal educational policies. I end this chapter by talking about the ideological component of language. Specifically, I show how language can be used, through texts, to misrepresent the "other" and also how it can be used as a tool of resistance to counter all forms of oppressions.

In chapter four, "Intellectuals: The Redefinition of Their Roles in a Neocolonial and Post-enlightenment Era," I analyze the ways in which intellectuals have impacted the world. I use as a building block the enlightenment movement to demonstrate how progressive ideas, such as justice, liberty, equality, and fraternity, which Voltaire and David Hume fought for, have mainly served the interest of the dominant European and colonizing class. I argue that their novel and revolutionary ideas did not serve the interest of the colonized Haitians and oppressed Indigenous people in South and Central America. Thus, given the hypocritical nature of the Enlightenment movement and its continued impact on neocolonized countries, I interrogate what is or what should be the role of restern intellectuals and allies vis-à-vis such a situation. After establishing the difference between conservative and borderless intellectuals I go further, suggesting that restern intellectuals should play the role of cultural vanguard in the fight against the economic exploitation, the cultural invasion of their countries, and the servile assimilation of the youth into western imperial culture.

In chapter seven, "Restern Women under Western Gaze: A Critical Sociohistorical Analysis of Their Struggles from the Colonial to the Neoliberal Era," I contextualize and analyze factors (historical, socio-economic, cultural, and political) that have shaped subjectivities, living, and working conditions of women, particularly women in the restern world. I demonstrate how, the legacy of slavery and colonialism combined with western neoliberal economic policy, have impacted restern women. I go on providing an overview of major assumptions that have been made about these women. Specifically, I show how some western researchers have constructed restern women's multifaceted realities as though they were homogenous. I challenge and reject such a misrepresentation arguing that it fails to fully capture the multiplicity of restern women's lived experience. I conclude this chapter demonstrating how researchers' political research agenda can influence the outcome of their research and lead to the misrepresentation of their informants.

In chapter nine, "Resterners' transnational migration to the West: What is at stake?," I explore the connection between the migration of many neocolonial subjects to western lands, such as the United States, France, and Great Britain, and the political and economic aggressions of these imperial powers against neocolonized countries. I go further using my immigrant experience in the U.S. as a cornerstone of analysis to explain how many neocolonial subjects, who have been forced to leave their native countries, felt caught between the West and the Rest, i.e., their native lands. I argue that they have experienced this feeling of being caught between these two worlds because of discriminations and socioeconomic exploitations they have experienced in the West and the nostalgia they have experienced leaving behind their beloved country of origin. I provide an analysis of various discriminations, such as racism, linguicism, and xenophobia, these postcolonial subjects and immigrants have faced in the West because of their nationality, religion, race, ethnicity, and language. Finally, I draw a parallel between these immigrants and other marginalized groups such as African Americans, Chicano/as, and Native Americans. Through this parallel, I demonstrate how the U.S. political system is set in a way that marginalizes and discriminates against people of color, particularly immigrants of color.

In the last chapter, "The Rest Inside the West: Haiti vs. New Orleans during Katrina," I begin with a comparison that a commentator made between New Orleans and Haiti after the Hurricane Katrina that destroyed New Orleans. Referring to New Orleans during Katrina, the American commentator said something along those lines: *Is this the United States of America? These images remind me of Haiti. This is not acceptable.* I challenge such a comparison theorizing that Katrina is a compelling evidence that the restern world exists within the western world. I unravel and analyze similar racial, socio-economic, and political factors that have impacted both people in New Orleans, which is one of the States the U.S., and people in the restern world, such as Haiti. My whole argument in this chapter is that Katrina should serve as a reminder to both westerners and resterners that the war of poverty that neocolonial and neoliberal western governments have been perpetrating against poor people does not exempt any of them, whether they are living in the western or in the restern world.

IMAGINE THE LIFE OF THE NEOCOLONIZED IN THE RESTERN WORLD.

I wish to begin this chapter with a poem that I wrote about a year ago on the socio-economic and political plights of poor people living in the restern world. In this poem, which I entitled *IMAGINE a COUNTRY*, I raise issues that often do not get to be discussed in school and through the mass corporate media. In using this poem as a preamble to this chapter, I hope it will resonate to the reader who might have witnessed and/or experienced some of what is being described in it. For those who cannot see themselves through this poem because their life experience has been different, I hope its content will make them critically reflect on their unearned privileges. My contention is that through critical reflection people develop critical consciousness which, in turn, might empower them to take action against inequalities of which many people, especially people in the restern world, have been a victim.

IMAGINE A COUNTRY

IMAGINE a country, where you were born and grew up, that has approximately 85% of its inhabitants who do not know how read and write; where schools are a luxury for millions of its people; where the school system is still operating among the debris of colonialism.

IMAGINE a country that is devastated by poverty and divisions among politicians who are obsessed with power, wealth, and fame; where children and innocent people are killed on a daily basis; where the legal system is controlled by the powerful, and functions for them alone.

IMAGINE a country where the majority of its people have to struggle daily for a single meal, while a small privileged class is living a luxurious life; where thousand of people are homeless and children are dying of hunger, malnutrition, and pollution, while large amounts of money are spent to buy or make weapons to kill innocent people and maintain the status quo.

IMAGINE a country where millions of people do not have access to clean, safe water; where children die of diarrhea caused by this water and other curable diseases; where the majority of people do not have health care; where the environment is constantly under attack.

IMAGINE a country where young beautiful women are the sexual objects of men, especially wealthy men; where young girls are sexually harassed, raped, and beaten by these men; where being a man is defined as having three or more women to treat as subalterns.

IMAGINE a country where women are overworked and underpaid in foreign owned factories; where they produce brand clothes and shoes like NIKE for 50 cents per hour, and yet do not earn enough money to feed themselves and their families.

IMAGINE a country where the wealthy or those with some kind of economic capital treat domestic workers, maids as modern house slaves; where politicians and other so-called leaders arm teenage boys and use them to murder their opponents as a way to stay in power.

IMAGINE a country where human rights are a meaningless concept for those in power and those who are simply armed; where speaking out against torture and governmental corruption is taken as a threat and can cost one's life.

IMAGINE a country from which you hold your most cherished memories; where your friends and family live, but which you hope to leave soon because of poverty, violence, and abuse of human rights.

IMAGINE a country where you are fearful and feeling unsafe because your political stance and ideology are taken as too subversive; where challenging the status quo equates to being a traitor, unpatriotic.

LOCATING MYSELF: A PERSONAL NARRATIVE OF A NEOCOLONIAL SUBJECT

Like many people in the restern world, I do not have to imagine the sad and ugly scenes described throughout this poem. Growing up in the poorest neocolonized country in the western hemisphere, Haiti, I personally experienced and witnessed some of these scenes, which might be the reality of people living in other parts of the world. Given my social class background, I was not expected to go to and finish high school, let alone to go to college and attend graduate school. Instead, like some of my neighbors, I was expected to follow my father's footsteps to becoming a carpenter, or else a poor farmer who is forced to sell his labor to a "grandon" (Haitian people who own a lot of lands and have many other assets besides), get a wife and some mistresses, grow old, and die poor. Or alternatively I could have become a soldier like my father at one point wished for me, a tailor like some of my neighbors, a bus driver, or a seasonal worker who does manual jobs here and there for survival. Or, like thousands of young Haitians, I could have become a "tonton macout" (Duvalier's private army) who tortured people who spoke against the Duvalier regime.

Out of the hundreds of people with whom I grew up, I was one of the few who made it through high school, to which millions of poor Haitians do not have access. In fact, in some rural areas, including the one where I spent part of my childhood, attending enough school to learn the basic reading and writing skills remains a dream for thousands of poor Haitian children. Some of these children had to work long hours on farms owned by power brokers who stole lands from the poor Haitian peasants who could not afford to send their children to the local school. Though I am the youngest in my family, I was the first child to graduate from high school and go to college. My older sisters were supposed to graduate high school before me but they did not make it beyond eighth grade. My father did not support the idea of investing in my sisters' education, fearing that they would get pregnant before graduating high school. In fact, my father was not alone in being reluctant to invest in his daughters' education. Many fathers believe that girls should get some basic education and then stay home to help their mother clean, cook, and take care of their younger brothers and sisters. Although this might not reflect the reality of middle and upper middle class Caribbean women, it remains a fact that sexism affects most, if not all, women in the Caribbean.

When I graduated high school at the age of 22, it was a dream come true for my semi-illiterate mother who sacrificed everything to support me throughout my high school years. I remember how proud she was to tell her friends, "My son just graduated from high school." However, the concept of college was foreign to my mother who had not gone beyond sixth grade. When I told her that I was applying for college, she replied: "I thought you were done with school, my son; when will you be done with school so that you can get a job to help me?" Though disappointed that I was not done yet with school, my mother continued supporting me through college hoping that I would find a job after I graduate. Unfortunately, I never got a job like my mother had hoped until after I left Haiti.

My high school and college years within a neocolonial school system were shadowed by political turmoil that paralyzed the whole country. However, until I became politically aware of this, I lived an innocent, naïve, and laissez-faire life style in my native country. I did not realize to what extent this country was devastated economically and politically by internal divisions that resulted from bloody fights among leaders in constant fight for power. Nor did I realize to what extent it was also economically and socially deteriorated by imperialist manipulations coming from western countries, such as France and the United States.

The reason I was able to live such an innocent and naïve life was that I did not have the political awareness and consciousness to question what I was taught to be natural and canonical truth. Until I started to question the [dis] order of things, I was regarded and treated as a good boy: obedient, smart, and polite. However, when I began asking pertinent or threatening questions about the Haitian school system that was colonial based then, and most likely still is, my high school teachers, some of my classmates, and others labeled me as an angry, atheist, a rebel, and a confused boy. In school, my classmates and I were not expected to ask too many independent-minded questions that would oblige our teachers to tell us the truth or challenge them to help us answer the following questions:

1. Why do students living in formerly colonized countries have to use textbooks and colonial masterpieces, whose content is culturally and historically alienating to them?
2. Why are French and English the primary languages of instruction in school rather than the local dialect and/or Creole, the native language of many students?
3. Why are professors who always speak French and standard English in class are considered "smart," "sharp," and "stylish," whereas those who dare use Creole or the local dialect as the instructional language are considered less intelligent by students, colleagues, and by administrators of the school?

4. Why do western neocolonizing imperial powers always feel they can intervene in times of "political crisis" and during electoral periods in restern countries attempting to control the political affair of these countries?
5. Why do farmers feel it is pointless to grow rice, corn, and beans because of an overflow of these products in their native land imported from the West?

Spending about two years in college in my native land did not enable me to develop a critical mind so I could answer the questions posed above. My colonial based schooling experience did not enable me either to understand the western cultural, political, and economic assaults against the restern world. I had to dig into the works of authors, such as Frantz Fanon, Amical Cabral, and Albert Memmi, to make sense of and critique what I was not allowed to know and question, that is, the imperialist interference of western countries in political affairs in and the continued negative effects of colonialism on restern countries.

Furthermore, my high school and college experiences within a colonial based school system did not teach me that growing up in an uneducated and poor family should not dictate one's destiny. Nor did these experiences teach me that being poor should not prevent one from questioning why restern countries have been put in a political and economic situation where they always have to rely on the western world for foreign aid or worse, borrow money from the International Monetary Fund (IMF) and the World Bank with exorbitant rates. Nor did my high school diploma and my three semesters at the Haitian State University equip me with the necessary critical and political consciousness to understand why factory workers worked long hours making shirts, pants, jackets, shoes, baseball, and football equipment for corporate capitalist interests while they could not feed or clothe their children, let alone send them to school. Noam Chomsky (1999) through his scholarly work has unveiled the cruel working working conditions of Haitian factory workers. Referring to the poor Haitians Chomsky (1999) argues that:

> Foreign-owned assembly plants that employ workers (mostly women) at well below subsistence pay under horrendous working conditions benefit from cheap electricity, subsidized by the generous supervisor. But for the Haitian poor-the general population-there can be no subsidies for electricity, fuel, water, or food; these are prohibited by IMF rules on the principled grounds that they constitute 'price control.'(p. 34).

What Chomsky describes above reflects the sad reality of neighbors and relatives in the neighborhood where I grew up. I remember my neighbors and relatives having to work ten to twelve hours a day, and yet they frequently had to borrow money from other neighbors and family members to feed their children and pay their bills. Selling their labor force for hours in the foreign-owned assembly plants did not enable them to improve their living conditions. On the contrary, these conditions had gotten worse from weeks to weeks until they were sent home after the closure of these assembly plants. Even though I was then a young boy, it was not too hard for me to make sense of their miserable conditions. Their tired and miserable looking face combined with their sad stories about their job were the vivid testimony of their inhuman working and living conditions.

Reflecting on the horrible working conditions of my neighbors and relatives I now realize that taking action against social injustice and inequality that permeate the restern world requires first and foremost lived experience and some form of education, but not necessarily formal schooling and a diploma obtained from a school system that is functioning among the debris of a school system that the colonialist left behind more than hundred years ago. As a high school student, I abhorred school. However, I never questioned the high intrinsic value of education although I have always believed it is not the product symbolized by a series of letters that one calls "Ph.D." or a piece of paper called a diploma, although those are vitally important acquisitions for obtaining social mobility, are personally and humanly gratifying, and can wisely be used to effect social change. Moreover, I have never believed that education is to be found only in school and received from professors. It also comes from a self-discovery. Such a self-discovery, I believe, can be obtained by reading various literatures, dialoguing, and co-constructing knowledge with others. I shall elaborate on this later in chapter four.

RESTERN COUNTRIES AT THE CROSSROAD OF WESTERN GLOBALIZATION:
THE HAITI CASE

Living in a poor, neocolonized country is a daily struggle for survival, especially for those who have been socially and economically marginalized by virtue of their social class and family background. As a young boy, I witnessed and personally experienced the rampant poverty that my neighbors and friends endured as a result of the political instability and terrible economic situation in Haiti. For example, in the neighborhood where I was born and grew up people had to walk miles to look for water, which often was neither clean nor safe. Medical doctors and clinics were nowhere to be found in the area. In case of emergencies, ambulances were unavailable, so people literally had to rely on unreliable public transportation and donkeys to get to the hospital located miles away from their house. Because of a lack of social and medical infrastructure available in their hometown, thousands of people have lost their lives when their lives could have easily been saved.

As for the farmers in my neighborhood, they lost hope after waiting for months for the rainy season to come so that they could continue growing sweet potatoes, rice, bananas, sugar cane, and corn to feed their families. The advance of science did not work for these farmers, who relied heavily on good rainy seasons to grow enough food to survive. Faced with the threat of famine and hunger, most of them ended up cutting down trees to make charcoal to sell to sustain themselves and their families financially. This desperate action taken by the farmers worsened their situation since there can be no rainy season without the protection of the environment.

When it rained, the farmers produced the agricultural products mentioned above in abundance, but the biggest problem they faced was that they were unable to compete with the imported western products on the market that were a lot cheaper than those they spent months growing. For example, since the Haitian meat, rice, and coffee have been devaluating, the poor had no choice but to buy the much cheaper imported products from the U.S., France, and Canada. Consequently, poor Haitian farmers found themselves increasingly financially bankrupt and unable to send their children to school as their crops remained devalued on the market. Meanwhile, members of the wealthy class, which constituted approximately 5% of the Haitian population, could easily afford to feed their children and send them to private schools. They were and still are the ones who have been in favor of western form of globalization through which they have maximized their profits. They have maximized their profits by buying in great quantity and selling imported products from the West on the Haitian Market. The poor Haitian farmers, on the other hand, did not and still do not have the economic capital to purchase these imported products which have been imposed on them to consume at the expense of the limited agricultural products they managed to produce.

Furthermore, in the 1980's the Haitian farmers experienced a drastic economic crisis when, following the pressure from western countries, such as the United States, thousands of Haitian pigs were slaughtered, though this was done under the pretext that the pigs were contaminated. The hegemonic truth behind this sordid action was that the United States needed an empty and available market to sell its own pigs, which the farmers could barely care for. Unlike the Haitian indigenous pigs that could eat anything and did not require any special food regiment to grow and be healthy, the imported pigs required special treatment and food. These pigs therefore became an economic burden to the poor Haitian farmers who had no choice but to pay for the special food regimen that these pigs required. The money that they spent on this special food regiment could have been used to feed their children who were starving.

In the countryside of Haiti, breeding indigenous pigs was the only source of revenue for the farmers who were deprived of social services, such as Medicaid and Medicare that are available for example in the United States. Breeding pigs constituted a form of financial banking centered on bartering. That is, when they needed money to purchase food, clothes, medication, and pay for their children's school tuition, they sold their grown pigs. It was not difficult to sell these pigs on the market because buyers were eager to buy animals they could take care of easily. However, selling the imported pigs was and still is a challenge for the Haitian farmers because consumers were extremely reluctant to buy these high-maintenance pigs.

Decimation of the indigenous pigs was not the only economic blow or disaster to hit the Haitian farmers. The indigenous roosters, hens, cows, and turkeys that they owned and depended on for survival were under attack as a result of western globalization. It was and might still be the norm to sell the imported products on the Haitian market in great quantity; no restriction from the Haitian government was imposed on the invasion of foreign meat. To put it simply, the imported roosters, hens, chickens, and turkeys from foreign countries, such as the United States, dominated every corner of the Haitian economy and market. Needless to say, the Haitian farmers could not compete with the flow of these imported meats, and their social and economic situations worsened as a result.

This kind of hegemonic interference affected not only Haiti's economy but also its culture. For example, as one of the components of the Haitian culture, I observed young and older Haitian people taking pride in wearing authentic Haitian clothes. My parents have always worn handmade clothes, and when I was a teenager, they always took me and my siblings to a Haitian tailor to have our clothes made for either school uniforms or other purposes. Making and wearing authentic Haitian clothes was very popular among the people, especially among members of the middle and working class. There were many tailors throughout my neighborhood, and they took pride in their work, which they depended on to feed their family and send their children to school. Haitian farmers were their most reliable and frequent consumers. Making and wearing authentic Haitian clothes greatly contributed to a sense of unity and community among the Haitians. As a result of their constant transaction and interaction, Haitian farmers and tailors developed a sound rapport with each other in the community. Although there was a lot of competition among the Haitian tailors to make the best possible authentic Haitian clothes, this did not prevent them from being bound by the sense of community created by their shared craft.

Practically all of this was destroyed when the Haitian market was bombarded by second or third hand clothes coming from neocolonizing countries, such as the United States and France, as part of their hegemonic ethos of globalization. Like the Haitian farmers, the Haitian tailors could not compete with this new imperialist cultural invasion. As a result, most of them involuntarily retired from the profession that had previously enabled them to feed themselves and their children for decades. Unemployed, they had no alternative but to migrate to Port-au-Prince, the capital of Haiti, in search of jobs that were already scarce. From this group of tailors and farmers forced to leave the countryside, some became thieves and criminals and are now among those manipulated and paid by politicians hungry and thirsty for power to commit unspeakable crimes and acts of violence.

The flood of used clothes from foreign countries has not only increased the level of poverty among the Haitians, but it also created competition and division among them. For example, those who wore and took pride in wearing the imported used clothes tended to believe that these clothes were superior to the authentic Haitian clothes. In fact, they tended to look down on the very small group of Haitians who, despite the influx of foreign cloth, clung to wearing the Haitian made clothes. Haitian teenagers were and still are the most common consumers of these second hand foreign cloths. For example, some of my high school classmates never hesitated to say that the authentic Haitian clothes were old- fashioned while they bragged proudly about the used brand name clothes, such as Nike, Tommy Hilfiger, and Polo attire, they wore.

On a recent trip to Haiti, I witnessed that it is not only second–hand clothes and imported food that dominated the Haitian market, but virtually everything one can conceive of, such as (1) used cars that are not allowed to be driven in the U.S. for legal and environmental reasons; (2) over the counter medications, and (3) canned foods that have expired. Friends and family members shared with me anecdotes about people who died as result of consuming and using products that were contaminated and expired. These are human tragedies that are not reported by the media, which is owned by corporate capitalists. Foreign imperialist countries, which are responsible for the human misery of the Haitian people, have remained largely silent and obviously have no interest in forestalling their criminal actions. What these imperialist countries are concerned about is finding cheap and convenient markets to unload and sell products that should have been disposed of.

The resources of a country include not only its people but also its environment. Thus, destroying the environment of any country leads to the destruction of the country's very structure so vital to the people who reside there. One of the major problems that restern countries have been grappling with is the attack by internal and external forces on their natural habitat leveled. As previously mentioned, poor Haitian peasants, forced by poverty and unaware of the importance of protecting the environment, have been cutting down trees to produce the charcoal they need to survive. Because of a lack of proper irrigation and the destruction of trees in the mountainous areas, some cities in Haiti have been devastated each time the country experienced natural disasters, such as hurricanes and major floods. A prime contemporary example was the flood in 2004 that destroyed plants, houses, and caused thousand of deaths in Haiti. However, the most drastic effects on the environment in Haiti was the toxic waste that the government of the United States dumped several years ago in *Gonaive*. If the whole continent of Africa, South and Central America, and Asia have been used by western researchers and scientists to conduct their research and scientific experiments, Haiti has become, thanks to its convenient location, the dumpster into which the US empire disposes of its toxic products and garbage.

HAITI UNDER THE EYES OF THE WEST

Haiti has been inscribed in the world historical archive as the first black nation that vigorously fought for and gained its independence, thereafter galvanizing the whole western hemisphere and helping other countries, such as Venezuela, to gain their independence. Since then, Haiti has been harshly punished, used, and exploited by the West. First, it was severely punished by the West for being the first black nation that dared to commit the "sin" of killing its White French colonizers to gain its independence. Such action thus threatened powerful western countries that were determined to prevent any radical grassroots movement from developing in the whole western hemisphere and elsewhere in the world. Second, as J. Michael Dash (1988) clearly explained in his book, *Haiti and the United States: National Stereotypes and the Literary Imagination*, Haiti has been paying a price for the significance of its past, and it is a price motivated by racism and the economic and political control held over the world by western imperial powers. And third, since its independence in 1804 Haiti has been under siege by, for example, the United States, which had occupied it for 19 years; controlled its political apparatus and its economy; and exploited its resources. As Dash (1988) points out, "Almost from the moment Haiti gained its independence as a Black republic in 1803 Americans tended to imagine it as a void into which they could pour their own ideas" (p.22).

Dash goes on to add "The United States occupied the Island in 1915 and set in place a native tyranny that exacerbated an already desperate state of affairs" (Dash cited by Said, 1993, Culture and Imperialism, p.289). And "when in 1991 and 1992 thousands of Haitian refugees tried to gain entry into Florida, most were forcibly returned" (Said, 1993).

Like many countries in Africa, Haiti does not seem to be a country to which the West pays close attention, precisely because (1) the majority of people living in it are poor and black and (2) there are no "communist or terrorist movements" taking place there. The only time the West pays attention to the political situation of Haiti is when there is a grassroots movement that threatens western imperialist interest. This has been the policy of the West towards Haiti for decades. Nothing has changed substantially in Haiti since its independence; almost everything remains the same, though with different political and economic masks.

Although Haiti is still used for geopolitical and economic reasons, it is no longer the convenient and beautiful Tropical Island it used to be. Nor is it the neocolonial island where white American and European tourists used to go for vacation and expected the local people to treat them as their modern white masters by preparing and serving them fine Haitian dishes, entertaining them with Haitian traditional music and dance, and by giving them lots of good sex. Nor is it the neocolonial island where so-called white European and American Christian missionaries loved to go to and be treated as kings and queens by the local people whom they taught Christian dogmas. To be precise, while sexually taking advantage of young Haitian girls and adults, these white missionaries-whom I would call neocolonizers-were preaching them the western model of the Gospel, which has been used as an ideological tool to westernize and oppress people living in the restern world.

As a young boy not yet able to understand the privilege of whiteness, I assumed, like every innocent Haitian child, that the people in my neighborhood were simply being hospitable to those white missionaries. What I failed to understand was that there was more to it than hospitality. The young adult Haitian males, who had some schooling, spent days practicing a song written in the neocolonizers language, English, as a way to welcome them in my native land. Within this same old church building, there was a kindergarten school where I received my first formal education. The Haitian female farmers, on the other hand, missed days of work to prepare the finest Haitian food in order to impress the white Christian European/American missionary men, who raped their teenage daughters, nieces, and other young girls in the neighborhood. The sad reality was that some Haitian parents knew that their teenage daughters were sexually molested by the white Christians, but did not take any action to stop this criminal act. On the contrary, it was discovered that most of them wished that their daughters got pregnant by the white men who, so they hoped, would "whiten" children in the family. Moreover, it was not a secret to the public that the same white Christian missionary men forced a lot of young Haitian girls to abort their children while they continued to have sexual relations with a few of them at the same time. Ironically, they were still getting the same respect that they got when they first invaded our neighborhood.

In terms of housing, there was no castle or mansion built for them in this impoverished neighborhood. However, the place where they stayed had what they wanted: respect, young girls, sexual gratifications, fine Haitian food and music. The life style of these white neocolonizers, in my opinion, was no different from that of the French colonizers in Algeria, Congo, and Tunisia; the Portuguese colonizers in Cape Verde and Mozambique; the British colonizers in Jamaica, Kenya, and Nigeria and the Spaniards in South and Central America and Mexico during colonization.

They seized our indigenous women from us and enjoyed the finest food that we did not have access to in our own land. In a word, they monopolized everything in the name of the Gospel and their whiteness and, before departing the country, they left us with a bible, written of course by their white ancestors and whose content could not help us liberate ourselves from mental slavery, neocolonial exploitation, and exploitative conditions. Instead, with this white bible the white missionaries/neocolonizers simply taught us to pray, pray, pray, forgive, forgive, forgive, love, love, love our enemies, but nothing about standing up to fight for our inalienable rights and change our poor social and economic conditions. They taught us to keep hoping for a better life in heaven, while on earth we were starving, oppressed, exploited, and discriminated against. Having witnessed and experienced the hypocrisy of and lies told by these white missionaries/neocolonizers, I quickly realized that this "white bible" would not do us any good. It simply taught us to be submissive and accept our horrendous socio-economic situations caused by the economic greed of western neocolonial powers and the dominant class in Haiti. To simply put it, we were duped and lied to by the white European and American missionaries/ neocolonizers who were preaching us a Gospel of submissiveness, of false hope, and of blind resignation.

CHAPTER 2

THE RESTERN WORLD

From Western Colonial to Western Neocolonial Domination

As I shall be using the term, "imperialism" means the practice, the theory, and the attitudes of a dominating metropolitan center ruling a distant territory; "colonialism," which is almost always a consequence of imperialism, is the implanting of settlements on distant territory.

Edward E. Said, *Culture and Imperialism*

Imperialism has been the most powerful force in world history over the last four or five centuries, carving up whole continents while oppressing indigenous peoples and obliterating entire civilizations.

Michael Parenti, *Against Empire*

Colonialism denies human rights to human beings whom it has subdued by violence, and keeps them by force in a state of misery and ignorance that Marx would rightly call a subhuman condition

Jean P. Sartre, in Memmi, *The Colonizer and The Colonized*

Being born and raised in a country with a history of colonialism is one of the greatest challenges that descendants of formerly colonized countries have to face. The reason is that the shadow of colonialism is deeply imprinted on their psyche and human consciousness and follows them throughout their journey in life. In fact, the legacy of colonialism overshadows the multi-faceted aspects of "postcolonial" subjects' ways of living and being in the world. In this sense, it is reasonable to argue that "postcolonial" subjects are in the best position to know how it feels to be post-colonized and cope with the aftermath and legacy of colonialism, such as continuous overt or subtle political and economic dominations of their native land, their misrepresentation and the misrepresentation of their culture and history. In the *Colonizer and the Colonized,* Albert Memmi (1965) brilliantly dissected the structure of the colonial system. He analyzed how colonialism dehumanized the colonized through brutal exploitation, subjugation, and misery. However, as Memmi made clear, the colonized were not the only ones who suffered from colonialism. The colonizers also suffered from it. They constantly feared that the colonized could violently revolt against the inhuman conditions they were forcibly put in by poisoning or brutally killing their colonizers. Thus, it can be argued that the colonial system rendered both the colonizers and the colonized its slaves. To para-

11

phrase Memmi, the so-called freedom that the colonizers enjoyed could only be maintained by sophisticated weapons, ideological brainwashing, and institutionalized fear. Psychologically they were not free; they were just as enslaved as the colonized.

Memmi's economic and political analysis of colonialism is very insightful in that it can help one understand western neocolonialism. Although Memmi did not explicitly make any claim as to what would happen to formerly colonized countries decades after they were colonized, his ideas, as articulated through his book, were somewhat prophetic. The economic and political situations of colonized countries, as Memmi laid them out in his book, are not so different from the current economic, social, and political situations of countries, such as Haiti, Congo, and India. For example, during colonialism the economic system of these countries was dominated and destroyed by western imperial powers' economic policies. And currently with the rise of western neocolonial and neoliberal economic policy, implemented through the World Bank, the International Monetary Fund, and the World Trade Organization, the economic system of Haiti and India, for example, seems to be as bad as it was during colonization. As a result of the implementation of this policy in these countries, many Indian and Haitian farmers have been forced to abandon their farms. This has economically and psychologically affected both the Haitian and Indian farmers and their family. For example, according to Arundhati Roy (2006), sixty wives of Indian farmers have committed suicide because they were overwhelmed by the accumulated debt of their husbands who were forced out of work due to western neoliberal economic policy. Roy put it in those terms while she was commenting on George W. Bush's official visit in 2006 in India to sign an "economic deal" with the Indian government:

> But I must say that while Bush was in Delhi, at the same time on the streets there were -- I mean apart from the protests, there were 60 widows that had come from Kerala, which is the south of India, which is where I come from, and they had come to Delhi because they were 60 out of the tens of thousands of widows of farmers who have committed suicide, because they have been encircled by debt. And this is a fact that is simply not reported, partly because there are no official figures, partly because the Indian government quibbles about what constitutes suicide and what is a farmer (Roy, interviewed by radio hostess, Amy Goodman, May, 2006).

Roy's statement illustrates that colonization, through the western model of globalization, is still happening in formerly colonized countries, albeit manifested in different forms and shapes. It also can be inferred from her statement that western neoliberal economic agenda has mainly served the interest of already existing privilege groups in formerly colonized countries but not that of the poor farmers and factory workers. Thus, going back to and contextualizing Memmi's diagnosis of the situation of the colonized and their occupied territories, it seems fair to state that his diagnosis is still relevant today and will be relevant for decades to come unless neocolonial subjects, including intellectuals, align with the masses to combat western neocolonialism. Simply put, as long as western neocolonialism exists, restern countries will continue experiencing economic and political dominations. In fact, many formerly colonized countries have already been experiencing a new form of colonialism since their "independence." This new form of colonialism, which will be discussed further in the book, is perhaps worse than nineteenth century-colonialism, because although subtle at times, it is operational at all levels (e.g. political, social, economic, cultural, and ideological) in restern countries. It is worth emphasizing that Memmi's detailed and perspicacious descriptions of the political, economic, and social situations of the colonized still to a great extent reflect the political, social, and economic situations of the marginalized Haitians, Indians, Somalis, and Sudanese, among others. These neocolonized subjects have been deprived of basic human rights and needs, such as clean and safe water, food, and shelter, while living under the constant threat of imperial and neocolonizing powers, such as the U.S., Great Britain, and France.

People who have lived under colonialism and/or have to deal with the historical, political, social, cultural, and psychological effects of colonialism do not know what their lives would have been like if their countries were not colonized. But this might not even be relevant or important to them in the final calculation, for after experiencing colonization, what these people do know is the color and taste of exploitation and humiliation resulting from it. Memmi (1965) explains this colonial phenomenon in the following terms:

> We have no idea what the colonized would have been without colonization, but we certainly see what has happened as a result of it. To subdue and exploit, the colonizer pushed the colonized out of the historical and social, cultural and technical current. What is real and verifiable is that the colonized's culture, society and technology are seriously damaged. (p.114).

Placing Memmi's argument in the context of neocolonialism, I shall argue that the struggle for political, economic, and cultural autonomies of countries that were formerly colonized must go on even though these countries have been "independent" for decades. The reason is that, despite the fact that white colonial administrators are no longer present in the colony to defend the interest of their superior colonialists in the western metropolitans, formerly colonized countries are still under the gaze of western neocolonial powers. Arundhati Roy (2003) eloquently unravels this neocolonial phenomenon in most of her scholarly and activist work. Roy (2003) argues:

> This time around, the colonizer does not need a token white presence in the colonies. The CEOs and their men do not need to go to the trouble of tramping through the tropics, risking malaria, diarrhea, sunstroke, and an early death. They do not have to maintain an army or a police force, or worry about insurrections and mutinies. They can have their colonies and an easy conscience. "Creating a good investment climate" is the new euphemism for western repression. Besides, the responsibility for implementation rests with the local administration. (p. 17).

13

What Roy points out above reflects the sad political and economic realities of most-if not all- formerly colonized countries in Africa, Asia, Latin America, and in the Caribbean. Despite radical nationalist movements that emerged out of mass struggle to resist the hegemonic influence of the West on the Rest, the former still finds ways to control internal affairs of the Rest via manipulation of corrupt leaders. These corrupt leaders are often put in power to defend the interests of the West while the majority of people, including journalists, students, and factory workers, are being murdered, exploited, and oppressed. The assassination of the famous Haitian journalist, Jean Dominic, in 2000, is a case in point. (See the movie *The Agronomist*)

Like Memmi, Fanon (1963) addressed issues related to domination and oppression in the colonial context. In *The Wretched of the Earth,* Fanon (2003) clarified the source of the "pitfall of national consciousness," caused by a national bourgeois class. This bourgeois class uses "the working class of the towns, the masses of unemployed, the small artisans and craftsmen to line up behind its nationalist attitude" (Fanon, 2003) for its own political and economic gains. In other words, the bourgeois class uses the masses to take over the colonizer's political and economic positions and to defend its own interests. The current economic and political state of formerly colonized countries, such as Uganda, Haiti, Somalia, Zimbabwe, Congo, and Rwanda, is prime example of a national bourgeois class whose aim is to have access to and remain in power by using the masses.

After years of independence from the French and British colonial powers, these countries have been destroyed by the greedy elite who, in order to stay in power, have isolated and killed whomever was opposed to their hegemonic agenda and violent actions. Moreover, while in power this elite group has usually reproduced the same colonial practices of the colonizer, for its political agenda has been always to replace the colonizers, but not to change the status quo. Fanon observed (1963):

The national middle class, which takes over power at the end of the colonial regime, is an underdeveloped middle class. It has practically no economic power, and in any case it is in no way commensurate with the bourgeoisie of the mother country, which it hopes to replace. In its narcissism, the national middle class is easily convinced that it can advantageously replace the middle class of the mother country. (p.149).

As Fanon noted, being obsessed with power, the emerging middle class from a colonial state has only strived to have access to and remain in power. Given their opportunist and bourgeois attitude, members of this class throughout history have been known to be reactionary. Like the colonizers, this class, often supported by the West, has proven to be oppressive to the poor masses and its opponents while in power. Some Haitian leaders are perfect examples of this. As Chomsky (2002) observes, "The United States has been supporting the Haitian military and dictators for two hundred years-it is not a new policy."

Chomsky's statement illustrates a very important point that I wish to make here. It is no longer the French and the British who have been only oppressing and exploiting the Haitians, Ugandans, Sudanese, Zimbabweans, Somalis, and the Rwandans; but it is also the powerful Haitians, Ugandans, Sudanese, Somalis, and Rwandans who, carrying out the legacy of colonialism and executing the economic order of the West at the expense of the poor, are torturing and impoverishing their compatriots. The colonizers and occupying empires have "left" the formerly colonized land, but the powerless people living in it have been experiencing what I would call "intra-national colonization" by their own government, which has not proven thus far that they are ready and capable to govern and unite the nation. Being supported by and, in some cases, put in powers by former western colonial powers and imperial power such as the U.S., these so-called leaders have divided these poor countries into multiple hostile and antagonist groups. They have also worked tirelessly to serve and protect both the interests of the western imperial powers and their own.

By arguing that leaders in formerly colonized countries have not convinced the world that they are able and competent to govern, I do not intend here to justify the distorted view of the colonizers who, in order to maintain the colonial status quo, have repeatedly stated that the colonized people are not ready or able to govern and represent themselves and must therefore let the colonial power do it for them. Rather, I am arguing that the real and uncompromising leaders emerging from the mass, or what Gramsci (1971) called "organic intellectuals," have not had the chance to lead and govern their countries without being attacked or killed by visible and invisible imperialist forces coming from the West. A good example of this is the Congolese Prime Minister, Patrice Lumumba, who was assassinated by western imperial power due to his nationalism and autonomous political and economic decisions to serve his country. (See the movie *Lumumba*).

In *A Dying Colonialism (1965)* Fanon warned us, in a prophetic way, of the danger of having a nationalist bourgeois and elite government take control of the nation after independence. Having assessed the social and political situations of the colonized, Fanon explained what consequences would result from the deceitful and dishonest political acts of the elite if they ever took over power. Fanon eloquently articulates that the elite had no interest in protecting from the colonizers the inalienable rights of the poor farmers and peasants. On the contrary, like the colonizers, the elite had a lot to gain from torturing the poor in order to have access to power. Said (1993) brilliantly captured Fanon's argument when he argued, "The national bourgeoisies and their specialized elites, of which Fanon speaks so ominously, in effect tended to replace the colonial force with a new class-based and ultimately exploitative one, which replicated the old colonial structures in new terms" (Said, p.223).

As has been historically proven, the national elite's "false generosity" (Freire, 1970) would be soon unveiled during national liberation and independence. Once colonized countries gained their independence, the elite of these countries were the first to collaborate with the colonizers in order to have access to power while marginalizing the peasants, farmers, and the rest of the population. The Congolese dictator, Mobutu Sese Seko, is a case in point. With the help of the former colonial power, Belgium and the U.S., he overthrew and participated in the assassination of the populist Congolese prime minister, Patrice Lumumba, whom he succeeded.

15

While he was in power, he continued soliciting and receiving support from the Belgian government to maintain it. To stay in power, he murdered thousands of Congolese who opposed to his government, as demonstrated in the movie *Lumumba*. Similarly, in the context of the neocolonial era, the elite of invaded and occupied countries, such as Iraq and Afghanistan, tend to be the group of people that collaborate with western imperialist powers so they can have access to political and economic powers. Ruling with a western mind, this elite class has created space and paved the path for western empires to continue invading and, worse, westernizing the restern world.

THE WESTERNIZATION OF THE RESTERN WORLD

As has been amply documented, the neocolonizers have always tried to subjugate and put the formerly colonized countries in a subaltern position. To this end, neocolonizing powers like Great Britain, France, and now the United States have eagerly and tenaciously been trying to control the internal economic and political affairs of formerly colonized countries. What have been the consequences of such imperialist actions? This question can be answered by taking a close look at what the U.S. and its imperialist ally, Great Britain, have done to restern countries, such as Haiti, Pakistan, Afghanistan, and East Timor for decades. They have invaded, brutally exploited, and tried to impose their prefabricated notion of democracy on these countries. In some of these countries, such as Afghanistan and Iraq, they have been somewhat successful by putting in power a puppet government that has been defending their interest. Given such imperialist actions, it is clear that the ideological, political, and economic agenda of these western imperialist powers has been to westernize the restern world through their neoliberal policy of ideological, economic, political, and cultural dominations.

Westernizing the restern world is certainly not a new concept, for it has existed for centuries. However, its effect nowadays is more obvious than ever in formerly colonized countries, which dared to fight for and gain their independence from western countries like the Great Britain, France, and Spain. Before going any further to discuss the westernization of the world, I think it is worth asking oneself: What is the West? Let it be known and clearly articulated that it is a West that has been conquering the rest of the world for centuries and has been a champion of the exploitation of the poor; a West that has monopolized the keys to the most advanced and sophisticated technology so it can control the restern world; a West that should be held accountable for the poverty and human misery of restern countries, yet has gotten away with it without blame; a West that has been exploiting and trying to politically control the restern world in order to occupy the most powerful position in the world. Finally, this is a West that expects restern countries to go along with its economic policy of oppression and domination.

Returning to the attempt of the West to westernize the rest of the world, I shall argue that such policy aimed to control not only the political and economic aspects of restern countries but also their ideological apparatus. As Said (1993) put it, "Westerners may have physically left their old colonies in Africa and Asia, but they retained them not only as markers but as locales on the ideological map over which they continued to rule morally and intellectually" (p.25). Said's statement is quite revealing and speaks to imperialist powers' propaganda to ideologically influence and thereby control a great portion of the rest of the world. One of the arguments--which is loaded of their ideological agenda--that the US and British governments have often put forward to justify their invasion and occupation of other countries is that the United States and Great Britain are "civilized and democratic nations." Therefore, any country that is not "civilized and democratic" has to be civilized according to the United States and Great Britain's definition of these concepts. In other words, in the eyes of these neocolonial and neoliberal powers, the Western definition of democracy, liberty, and freedom is the best one and therefore must be embraced by "undemocratic and uncivilized" restern nations. Clearly the message that the West seems to be sending to the Rest is that "We westerners we will decide who is a good or bad native, because all natives have sufficient existence by virtue of our cognition. We created them, we taught them to speak and think, and when they rebel they simply confirm our views of them as silly children duped by some of their Western masters" (Said, 1993, xviii). One would, then, need to be politically naïve and uninformed to fail to understand that the hidden ideology behind these outright lies of the West is to economically, culturally, and politically dominate the Rest.

As U.S. imperialism has been trying to politically and economically control a great portion of the world, the West no longer encompasses only the British, French, and Spanish empires which, for decades, have colonized thousands of countries in Africa, the Caribbean, South and Central America. In other words, as Serge Latouche (1996) brilliantly put it

> The West no longer means Europe, either geographically or historically; it is no longer even a collection of beliefs shared by a group of people scattered over the earth. I see it as a machine, impersonal, soulless, and nowadays masterless, which impressed mankind into its service. This mad machine has shaken off all human attempts to stop it and now roves the planet, uprooting what and where it will: tearing men from their native ground, even in the furthest reaches of the world, and hurling them into urban deserts without any attempt to adjust them to the limitless industrialization, bureaucracy and technical 'progress' which the machine is pursuing. (pp. 4-5).

The concept "machine" that Latouche used in defining the West symbolizes, in my view, globalization and its catastrophic socio-economic and political effects. My argument is that globalization is in itself a machine that corporate western imperialist countries have been using to widen the gap between the haves and the have-nots, the privileged groups and the underprivileged groups, in restern countries. Globalization has probably caused more economic harm to countries in the restern world than any operational capitalist machine that western imperialist countries have historically used for gigantic profits. The supposed initial mission of globalization was to strengthen the economy of countries devastated by the Second World War, to create more jobs, and transport beyond borders goods and medical equipments from which people, especially the poor, could benefit. However, informed by western corporate capitalist agenda, globalization has drastically paralyzed the economy of poorest countries in the restern world. As the democratically elected president of Bolivia, Evo Morales, eloquently put it, "Globalization creates economic policies where the transnationals lord over us, and the result is misery and unemployment."(Morales, interviewed by Times magazine, 2006). As Joseph Stiglitz (2003) pointed out, one can only hope that,

> Globalization can be reshaped, and when it is, when it is properly, fairly run, with all the countries having a voice in policies affecting them, there is a possibility that it will help create a new global economy in which growth is not only more sustainable and less volatile but the fruits of this growth are more equitable shared. (p. 22).

Globalization is not a new economic and political phenomenon, for there has always been trade between countries. However, to paraphrase Kamat (2000) and Robertson (1992, 1997), through the western version of globalization, restern countries have simply been put under the siege of western economic expansion and exploitation. In fact, with its ruinous effects, globalization has profoundly impacted the economy of poor countries like Haiti, Bolivia, Guatemala, El Salvador, and India. Roy (2001), describes the impact of globalization on India in the following terms:

> From April 1, 2001, according to the terms of its agreement with the World Trade Organization (WTO), the Indian government will have to drop its quantitative import restrictions. The Indian market is already flooded with cheap imports. Though India is technically free to export its agricultural produce, in practice most of it cannot be exported because it does not meet the first world's "environmental standards." (You do not eat bruised mangoes, or bananas with mosquito bites, or rice with a few weevils in it...In effect, India's rural economy, which supports seven hundred million people, is being garroted. Farmers who produce too much are in distress, farmers who produce too little are in distress, and landless agricultural laborers are out of work as big estates and farms lay off their workers. They are flocking to the cities in search of employment. (pp.15-16).

As Roy's description of the horrible economic situation of India clearly indicates globalization is not the solution to the economic and social problems of restern countries. It has simply been used as part of the neocolonial and neoliberal agenda of United States, France, and Great Britain to continue exploiting their formerly colonized countries. Like the former white colonial administrators in the French and British colonies, the CEOs of the World Trade Organization (WTO), the World Bank (WB), and the International Monetary Fund (IMF) have local administrators in countries like Jamaica, India, and Haiti to defend the interests of these organizations. As Roy noted earlier, these CEOs do not have to be in these tropical countries and run the risk of getting malaria or other illnesses and deal directly with factory workers there. They can still make millions from these workers' sweat and blood without having to know who they are, let alone interact with them.

As the CEOs of these capitalist corporations intended to make the masses believe, it would be ideal if the objective of the IMF, the WTO, and the WB were to financially help restern countries to be economically stable. But rather their corporate agenda is to destabilize to an even greater extent the economy of these countries that depend on the backbone of farmers, who are unable to compete with the technological advances and the economic greed-driven attitude of western countries. Joseph E. Stiglitz (2003) puts it in these terms:

> Forcing a developing country to open itself up to imported products that would compete with those produced by certain of its industries, industries that were dangerously vulnerable to competition from much stronger counterpart industries in other countries, can have disastrous consequences-socially and economically. Jobs have systematically been destroyed-poor farmers in developing countries simply could not compete with the highly subsidized goods from Europe and America-before the countries' industrial and agricultural sectors were able to grow strong and create new jobs. (p. 17).

In addition to Roy's analysis of India's terrible economic situation caused by the western version of Globalization, Stiglitz's critique of this corporate capitalist machine makes clear that restern countries will get poorer and poorer as long as they continue signing diabolic economic contracts with the World Bank and the International Monetary Fund. Unfortunately, signing this kind of economic contract with these western organizations is a vicious economic cycle in which many restern countries have been forced and trapped. This vicious economic cycle has thus far been responsible for the chronic poverty of the poor in the restern world. I shall go further, arguing that the root of the political, economic, and social problems of these countries seems also to partially lie in the "economic and social Samaritan actions" of the West through non-governmental organizations in restern countries.

NGOS AND THE RESTERN WORLD

Colonialism has unquestionably paralyzed economically, politically, and even culturally restern countries. However, I shall assert that neocolonialism appears to be worse than colonialism because, though subtle, its devastating effects are enormous and unprecedented. Neocolonialism can be and is indeed implanted in neocolonized lands in such an invisible way that might not instantaneously provoke radical mass movements among those who have been marginalized and oppressed. In fact, neocolonialism has been used by western countries like a slow but an active economic and political poison pill administered by corporate organizations such as IMF, World Bank and, to a certain extent, the Non Governmental Organizations (NGOs) to which I am now turning my analysis.

Unlike the policies and regulations of International Monetary Fund (IMF) and World Bank that usually lead to instantaneous reactions from the poor, the NGOs have had an easier time being implemented in restern countries. The reason behind this seems to be that people in such restern countries as Haiti and India generally tend to believe that these organizations are aimed to helping the poor without any governmental influence. Consequently, the NGOs are perceived to be politically neutral and economically autonomous while carrying out their "Samaritan" or "humanitarian" mission. This perception and conception of NGOs has led some activists and intellectuals from the "left" to work with and/or for these organizations.

I am reminded when I was in High school, one of my teachers who was known to be a leftist worked for an NGO for years. Through his daily rhetoric he never hesitated to speak in favor of this organization. In fact, he took pride in being one of the representatives of this organization. My teacher's rhetoric about his affiliation with the NGO was so convincing and his influence was so strong that I felt the burning desire to work for this "great organization," as he usually put it. I at the time thought that working with or for this organization would enable me to help the poor without having to deal with the politics of governmental deceit. Thus, my goal after high school was to work for a NGO while pursuing a college degree. However, what my teacher failed to explain was that, although there might be some NGOs that contribute to some kinds of social change, this organization has not yet proven to be capable of helping eradicate chronic social, economic, and political problems that have sabotaged restern countries.

Although NGOs to a certain extent might have helped certain social institutions in poor countries remain functional, they simultaneously constitute a barrier to radical social, political, and economic changes in these countries. The reason is that real social and political changes cannot take place without attacking the political apparatus that holds power and privilege and that defines how this privilege and power should be distributed. Yet, as a politically and governmentally "neutral" organization, NGOs do not seem to have any interest in speaking to power. Therefore, it may be argued that these organizations are in direct or indirect complicity with governments that are hostile to radical social and political changes. In fact, the very existence of NGOs in restern countries works to the advantage of the governments of these countries because these organizations can be used as a facade to mask a country's lamentable economic and social state and the misery of the poor. Hence, from a radical vantage point, one might argue that NGOs are a part of the western neocolonialist agenda that operates in a subtle way.

By making this argument, I am not suggesting that NGOs should be fought against like neocolonialism should, as some NGOs have somewhat contributed to certain types of social change, such as providing some training to social services workers and opening cultural centers for young people. However, my argument is that if NGOs are really serious about effecting social change, they must begin by finding ways in which to influence the political force of the countries where they are operating. One of the ways this can be done is to help the youth and students be aware of and active in the political affairs of their own countries. Failing to do this, NGOs will simply help maintain the status quo in restern countries.

With that said, I suggest that NGOs should be restructured in order to become part of the organizational machine that runs for social justice and social change in restern countries. For example, in Haiti one of the major things that needs to be changed within these organizations is their bureaucratic structure and thus the parasitic and opportunistic attitude of their employees. Among these employees, one finds college students, professors, and the so-called leftist intellectuals who only see NGOs as a way to fill up their pockets and embellish their resumes, rather than an organization through which they can work to effect social change. It goes without saying that corruption from within NGOs is rampant, although it might not be as visible as the corruption that ruins the governmental and political structures of restern countries.

In short, to be effective and truly helpful to restern countries, NGOs need to be involved in and support the political struggle in which the poor have been engaged. Otherwise, these organizations will merely be a pill that temporarily relieves the pain of social and economic diseases of restern countries caused by the west, rather than being a part of the diagnosis and cure of these diseases. Finally, by failing to attack directly or at least point fingers at atrocities of governments that put restern countries in a state of political, social, and economic agonies and dependence, NGOs will continue to be accused of perpetuating the political and economic legacy of colonialism.

WESTERN HEGEMONIC CONTROL OF THE ECONOMIC AND POLITICAL STRUCTURES OF THE RESTERN WORLD

As previously noted, western neocolonizing countries have no other political and economic agenda for restern countries but to politically and economically paralyze them. To do so, they have been using all sorts of strategies. The most common strategy has thus far been invasion and occupation of these countries, which I shall talk about in depth in chapter four. When western neocolonizing powers cannot create a climate of terror and fear as an excuse to invade and occupy restern countries, they try to manipulate puppet political leaders to protect their corporate interest. In other cases, they train and finance death squad groups to oust or kill any democratic leader that refuses to obey to their political and economic dictates. Thereafter, they orchestrate a climate of terror aiming to justify their military intervention and invasion in these countries to supposedly help restore peace and order. The climate of economic and political terror, ignited by the U.S. that led to the overthrow of the Haitian President, Jean Bertrand Aristid, is a case in point. Trained and supported by these neocolonizing powers, a group of soldiers politically destabilized Haiti until Aristid was forced to leave the country in 1991. Immediately after his departure, the United Nations, following the orders of the U.S., sent a troop to "establish democratic order" in the country. I am convinced that the same troop could have been sent to counter the criminal action of these soldiers that helped to overthrow president Jean Berrand Aristid if he was serving the interest of the U.S., France, and Canada.

Alluding to western neocolonizing countries' rhetoric about promoting and maintaining democracy abroad, I wish to pose the following question: How can a country boastfully claim that its goal is to help restore democracy in other countries around the globe while people within its own borders are deprived of their democratic rights? Chomsky (1996) captures this hypocrisy when he argues:

A society that excludes large areas of crucial decision-making from public control, or a system of governance that merely grants the general public the opportunity to ratify decisions taken by the elite groups that dominate the private society and the state, hardly merits the term "democracy.

Elaborating on Chomsky's argument, I would contend that one cannot talk about a democratic society when the government of this society simply wants people to be spectators and followers of its political and economic decisions. Nor can one talk about democracy when it only satisfies and meets the needs of a small elite group. While the West has not proven that it can promote and maintain democracy and freedom in its own land, ironically it has been increasingly determined to export its so-called notion of democracy and freedom abroad. In its own backyard, immigrants and minority groups, such as African Americans, Black, Latino/as, South Asians, and people of Arabic descent have been unfairly jailed and tortured. Thus, one has to wonder if Western neocolonizing empires are not the most hypocritical empires that have ever existed on earth. For example, while unfairly arresting and brutalizing its own citizens who stand for workers', women's, and prisoners' rights and denying people of color access to decent housing, jobs, health care, and quality education, the West has been trying to sell its "banking concept" (Freire, 1970) of democracy and freedom to restern countries. This act in itself is the most convincing evidence that the West is very hypocritical in that it does not practice what it has been preaching to the restern world.

Despite the corporate media's attempt to cover up what happened in countries, such as Grenada, Panama, Guatemala, Chile, Haiti, Afghanistan, and Iraq, the informed citizens know what the West has done to these countries. They know that in 1982 the U.S. participated in the assassination of Maurice Bishop because he was defending his country, Granada, from US imperialism. They know that in 1990 the U.S. invaded Panama to capture its old protégé but rebellious friend, Manuel Noriega; in the Dominican Republic the U.S. supported the bloody dictator, Trujillo, who murdered thousands of poor innocent Haitians; in Guatemala in 1954 it participated in the overthrow of the socialist president, Jacob Albenz who was perceived as a threat to its interest; in 2003 the U.S. invaded Iraq for oil purposes; in Afghanistan in 2002 thousands of innocent children and elderly people lost their lives due to the U.S. invasion motivated by its search of Osama Bin Laden; in Chile in 1973 the U.S. plotted the overthrow of a popular socialist president, Salvador Allende; and finally, in Haiti in 1991 and 2004 the U.S. overthrew twice the democratically elected president, Jean Bertrand Aristide, who represented a threat to its interest.

These actions are undeniable proof that part of the neocolonizing agenda of western countries is to have a free zone for big corporate investments in and to gain political and economic control of restern countries. Said (2003) noted:

Everything is packaged and up for sale. This is the meaning of the neoliberal market economy, which globalization has foisted on the world, leaving very

little room for individual challenge and questioning, whereas large organizations, whether governments or corporations, pursue policies that are virtually
blind in many instances, causing widespread environmental destruction,
widespread genetic destruction, and the possibility for powerful groups to
pursue profit without responsibility. (p.99).

As Said's comment makes clear, what fundamentally interests western neocolonial
countries are their economic and corporate interests. The economic greed of Western imperialist countries becomes evident through their participation in assassinat-
ing political activists and ousting leaders in restern countries that represent a threat
to their corporate capitalist interests. Once their economic interest is in danger, it
does not matter if people are oppressed, starving, or killed.

Because of their economic greed, Western empires have been trying to put restern countries under economic and political siege for decades. Occupying colonial
forces may have been forced by grass-roots movements to leave formerly colonized and occupied countries, but they unquestionably left behind western-trained
national armies to protect their own corporate capitalist interests. In formerly colonized countries such as Haiti and Congo, among others, most of the presidents have
been generals or someone who was affiliated with the army of these countries. So
the colonial power, although not physically there, continues to control the political
structure of these countries through the army and with the complicity of corrupt
leaders and the elite. Presidents who have risen out of a mass popular movement
have either been ousted and/or killed by the yankee-army that has been put in place
by western neocolonizing countries. The short-lived presidencies of Salvador Allende in Chile, Patrice Lumumba in Congo, and Thomas Sankara in Grenada are
prime examples of this. However, presidents or, rather, dictators such as Duvalier
(Haiti), Trujillo (Dominican Republic), Pinochet (Chile), Mobutu Sese Seko
(Congo) have been protected by Western empires despite all the crimes they have
committed against their own people and humanity. Chomsky and Herman (1979)
cast some light on this historical fact. They state:

> The old colonial world was shattered during World War II, and the resultant
> nationalist-radical upsurge threatened traditional Western hegemony and the
> economic interests of Western business. To contain this threat the United
> States has aligned itself with elite and military elements in the Third World
> whose function has been to contain the tides of change. This role was played
> by Diem and Thieu in South Vietnam and is currently served by allies such as
> Mobutu in Zaire, Pinochet in Chile, and Suharto in Indonesia. (p.8).

As pointed out above by Chomsky and Herman, it is clear that the agenda of U.S.
imperialism is to protect its corporate interest in formerly colonized countries by
all means necessary. The complicity of the U.S. government in the assassination of
priests and poor farmers in countries, such as El Salvador and Nicaragua who stood
up against U.S. imperialism in the late 1970's and 1980's are cases in point. For
western imperial powers like the US, farmers and peasants are not human beings,
therefore they can be treated and killed like animals. Ironically, the killing of these
farmers has been done in the name of U.S. definition of freedom. In regard to this

hypocrisy, Chomsky (1996) righteously asks: "What kind of freedom is there inside a corporation?"

Chomsky's question is a valid one and speaks to the dominance of restern countries by western countries. Since their "independence," restern formerly colonized countries have been used by neocolonizing powers as convenient sites to build factories, where the poor provide cheap labor to make brand name shoes, shirts, pants, and baseballs to enrich the CEOS of these factories. These products have been made by Haitian, Indian, and Pakistani factory workers for say 25-50 cents per hour to be sold for a fortune in countries, such as the United States and France. For example, a pair of jeans made by a Haitian factory worker for 30 cents could cost between $ 25 and $ 80 in the United States. Chomsky (1994) described such a horrible situation as follows:

> Baseballs are coming along nicely. They're produced in US-owned factories where the women who make them get 10 cents an hour-if they meet their quota. Since meeting the quota is virtually impossible, they actually make something like 5 cents an hour. Softballs from Haiti are advertised in the U.S. as being unusually good because they're hand-dipped into some chemical that makes them hang together properly. The ads don't mention that the chemical the women hand-dip the balls into is toxic and that, as a result, the women don't last long at this work. (p. 78).

As Chomsky clearly describes it above, the western form of globalization has economically paralyzed poor Caribbean farmers and factory workers. Particularly in the case of Haiti, globalization has affected everyone; however, women have been the major victims of it. Haitian women have spent hours laboring for cheap prices in U.S.-owned factories. They barely have time to breast feed their babies. Even when they are sick they still have to go to work in these factories, for there is no law that obliges these foreign factories to provide health insurance and sick day benefits to Haitian women. However, this horrible working condition to which restern factory workers have been subjected in U.S.-owned factories unfortunately remains unknown to many people in the West because the western mass corporate media has too often covered it up.

Later in chapter seven, I shall talk in great details about the socio-economic conditions of women living in the restern world. I wish to end this chapter making the following points: (1) The so-called version of western democracy and neoliberal economic policies need to be questioned and fought against because they only serve the interest of western imperial powers. And (2) given the ruinous economic and political effects of western colonial and neocolonial policies on the restern world, it is imperative that what happens locally or nationally is linked to what happens internationally. Local/national and international politics intersect with and influence each other. Therefore, they should not be studied in a disconnected way. Failing to link the national to the global might prevent one from grasping that the western neocolonial model of globalization has affected poor people both nationally and globally.

NOAM CHOMSKY AND PIERRE ORELUS

A Dialogue about the Impact of Colonialism and Imperialism on Restern Countries

CONTEXT

The dialogue that follows took place between Noam Chomsky and Pierre Orelus on March 18, 2005, at Chomsky's office at the Massachusetts Institute of Technology. While writing some essays on the impact of globalization, imperialism, and the legacy of colonization on restern countries, I felt that, besides my lived experience with and information excerpted from books about these issues, it was imperative that I have insights from a critical analyst who has a keen understanding of how colonization, globalization, and western imperialism have negatively impacted restern countries' economic, political, and educational systems. To this end, I decided that I would try to interview one or two scholars who have written about or at least proven to be fully aware and well informed of Haiti's and other restern countries' economic, political, social, and educational situations. In my self-questioning, I could not think of any prominent thinker than Professor Noam Chomsky who, throughout his scholarly and human rights activist work, has brilliantly unmasked the imperial and neocolonial actions of western power against formerly colonized countries, such as Haiti and India. Thanks to his intellectual generosity, Professor Chomsky agreed to share with me his insights on the colonial, neocolonial, and Western imperialist actions on Haiti and other restern countries, such as India and Nicaragua.

As the reader will see through this informal conversation, Professor Chomsky starts by briefly talking about the history of colonialism and its negative impact on India and Haiti. He goes on to talk about western imperial actions against these two countries. In the case of Haiti particularly, Professor Chomsky talks about how the U.S. has been trying to control this country through political manipulation and economic exploitation. He gave concrete examples through the interview explaining how this has been done.

A detailed analysis of the dialogue that I engaged in with Professor Chomsky of course can be provided here. However, I thought it would be preferable to let the reader make sense of it him/herself. This interview was conducted in a very informal way. Thus, it may not have strictly followed the syntactical and grammatical conventions of what is called academic writing. Furthermore, while editing the transcription of this interview I made sure to do so in way that does not affect its originality. In other words, I made a conscious choice to leave intact interruptions and unfinished sentences, which normally occur during informal conversation. However, to clarify the context of and make the content of this dialogue accessible to the reader, I provided additional information in brackets and parenthesis.

[Here Chomsky started answering Pierre's question on the legacy of colonialism before he turned on the tape recorder; so some of what Chomsky said previously did not get recorded]

Chomsky: They (i.e., British colonizers) created a rich Indian elite; ...they did not call themselves collaborators, but they were basically running the country, and the British didn't have many troops there. They were running the country with Indian Sepoys and tribesmen. And the usual technique was to move them around, so you could use ethnic conflict and things like that, so the guys from one area would kill the people from the other area. In fact, the British colonization in most of the world; a lot of it was with Indian soldiers in Afghanistan, Africa, and so on. And if you take a look at post-colonial India...

Pierre : *Right...*

It is the typically the elites who came out of the British rule.

Pierre: *So would you agree....[Interrupts]*

Chomsky: And it is the same rhetoric. Actually there is a really good book on it if you have not seen it yet by...

P: *Who is the author?*

C: Do you know Basil Davidson?

Pierre : Yes, I do.

C: He's one of the leading historians of Africa and a very good one. He pays attention to Africa, and he has a book. I forget what it is called, but something like "Black Africa." It is about the post-colonial Black Africa. I mean he was really committed to the anti-colonial movements, and he was involved with them. He was kind of on the left. He was then very disappointed by what came out, but he describes it very honestly and accurately, and he knows the history.

P: *Ok. Let me see if I understand what you just pointed out. Referring to the colonial legacy of colonization on Third World countries such as Haiti, and all the conflicts, division, killings, and exploitation that Haiti has, you know, gone through, would you say this is the end result of colonization?*

C: It's not the end result; it is still going on. I mean Haiti is a particular, special case because the Haitian revolution in 1804, you know, when they finally won... I mean that revolution just terrified everyone in the world. The British, if I recall correctly, sent more troops to Haiti than they sent to the American colonies to prevent the rebellion. In fact, it was just - I am sure you know the history- it was just a combined effort of every imperial country in the world, including the U.S ... by then the former U.S. colonies, to crush the revolution because it was terrifying the idea that you know ... French sent a huge army; British sent a huge army; Spain Was involved; the US was involved. And it was particularly frightening for the United States of course because it was a slave society... Here's the first free country in the Hemisphere. They could not tolerate that. Well, I don't want to go on with stuff you know perfectly well. You know the French imposed a huge on indemnity on them (i.e., Haitians) to pay the cost of having liberated themselves. The U.S. agreed. In fact, U.S. did not recognize Haiti until 1862, when they recognized Liberia for the same reason…

P: *Right, right…*

C: Get rid of the slaves…

P: *Right, right…*

C: That's Abraham Lincoln… And then comes that hideous history of the … I don't want to go through it, but it goes right through to the present. I mean Clinton and the first Bush openly supported the military junta. I mean they were not reported here, but it was pretty obvious. They even went as far as authorizing illegal shipments of oil. They authorized Texaco to override presidential directives not to ship right in the middle of this war and while the CIA was testifying to Congress that no oil is being sent; well, you could see the ships in the harbor, building their oil platforms …It got leaked afterwards, but the press refused to report it. And right after the President Bush number two cancelled the aid.…

P: *It is obvious that imperialism and what I would call neocolonialism affects the political, social, and educational system of Haiti. But it seems to me they haven't really… people who are doing analysis on Haiti don't seem to focus much on the educational aspect of it. To me… [interrupts]. So would you agree that colonialism and imperialism or if you like neocolonialism affects the educational system of Haiti as much as its political, social, economic …*

C: I think that is typical of colonialism. So take again the British and India, a classic case. I mean they revised the whole education system and the idea was to train them to be loyal subjects to the crown. And there were elements in the Indian elites which benefited from this; the guys who ran it. So…in fact, if you take a look at any western country, I man a typical phenomena is that there is a sector that lives in enormous wealth, I mean way better than I do when I see when I visit them. It's kind of mind-boggling, but that's everywhere, and by now a lot of them are former revolutionaries because they feel they … that when you talk to them. Like, I was in South Africa a couple years ago, in Cape Town.

P: *Yeah, actually the stuff you…*

C: Did I talk about it?

P: *Yeah…you did in your talk*

C: Did I talk about meeting with the…

P: *Yes, you mentioned it…*

C: But that's typical. In Nicaragua, I've visited there for a long time; my daughter lives there with grandchildren and stuff, but the Sandinistas are the worst crooks around. And you can see why. I mean during the 80s, it was not entirely visible because since they were in the government, you could not clearly distinguish how much is just ripping of the population and how much is being in the government, so you have a big car you know, but as soon as they were out of the government, it becomes apparent. My daughter's companero (i.e., partner) that she lives with, his sister, poor woman, lives in a place right across the street from a huge walled estate. Nobody really knows what's inside, castles and baseball fields and so on.

27

That's owned by Umberto Ortega. He doesn't even bother living there; he lives in Costa Rica since it is nicer down there. I mean they just ripped off the whole country. I mean that is the same in South Africa; it is the same just in any colonial county you go to... I cannot think of any exception to that.

P: *As a Haitian immigrant living here...there is a question that kept coming to me since actually I moved here. People who seemed to be curious to know about what is happening in Haiti have asked me, for example, why would the U.S. be interested in Haiti? Why would they want to be involved in the political affairs of a poor country like Haiti. That's their argument...*

C: Now it's a poor country, it was the richest colony in the world...

P: I am referring to the current political and economic situations of Haiti.

C: Now, it's...Look...For a long time, I mean as late as when Woodrow Wilson invaded it, it was still a potentially wealthy country. It was not like it was under French. Maybe... a lot of French wealth comes from Haiti, but it had lasted until the early 20th century. I mean Wilson pretty much destroyed it. But even after Franklin Roosevelt destroyed a lot of Haitian agriculture to raise rubber because he needed rubber during the second world war, it was perfectly capable of raising rubber. [This was] terrible for the population – they needed food. And after the war, they just destroyed all, and it went on until the 1980s. I mean USAID, the U.S. aid system, in the early 1980s had plans for converting Haiti into what they called "Taiwan of the Caribbean." They were going to make assembly plants for really cheap labor for American corporations and so on, and it goes into the Clinton years. I mean when Clinton -and by now it is not going to be a rich country anymore: too much is destroyed by imperial violence, but as late as mid-90s, I mean when Clinton allowed Aristide to return, he insisted that Aristide accept the program and move out.

P: *Right, right...*

C: You know the defeated the U.S. candidate (i.e., Marc Bazin) in the 1990 election.... but the point was to destroy Haitian agriculture. I mean Haitian rice farmers are poor but they were very efficient. Obviously they cannot compete with highly subsidized U.S. agriculture, so opening the doors ... wiped out... could have been productive...

P: *I have...*

C: They even went to the extent of wiping out small industries, like they were a couple of small industries that were functional in Haiti, like chicken parts, which was working, but the trouble is that American big corporations like Tyson, Clinton's friend...; Americans don't like dark meat, so they have a huge excess of dark meat and they wanted to dump it somewhere. So they tried to dump it in Mexico and Canada, but they have laws. You know they have anti-dumping laws so they could not do it. However, Haiti under Clinton was forced to accept the condition on Aristide's return. There would be no conditions on imports, so his friends like Tyson could therefore dump chicken meat on Haiti and wipe out the chicken-parts industry, and it is not that the country in principle could not survive there... could...

P: *I actually have....*

C: Actually the same thing is happening with CAFTA right now. I mean you read the Boston Globe and they'll tell you that this is just going to be marvelous for Central America because they are going to have... but what they don't tell you is what every development agency knows including the NGOs that the right-wing criticize at the end...

But published reports like OXFAM ...published reports are saying that the first effect of CAFTA will be to drive tens of thousands of farmers off the field because it means that highly U.S. subsidized agriculture is going to wipe out poor farmers.

P: *I have a similar example to what you just pointed out. In the early or mid-80s, lots of indigenous pigs owned by Haitian farmers and peasants were killed by the Haitian government.....*

C: That was incredible. But that was at the orders of the United States! I mean the U.S. ordered them to kill the pigs on the basis of totally fraudulent claim about swine fever, but the point was to bring in pigs from Iowa – you know- which are fat, elite pigs; they have to be fed special diets that no Haitian farmer could possibly afford. I mean that would be more than their entire annual income to feed these stupid pigs. But they were brought in, and of course they could not survive, and meanwhile the Haitian pig culture was [destroyed], and it was more than just food; pigs were part of the culture, deeply embedded in the whole cultural system, and they were very hardy and resistant and they were something the poor farmers could use, so they had to be killed. If you ... it's kind of comparable to destroying social security here. I mean anything that is useful for poor people, like 90% of the population, anything that works for them is useless; so it has to be destroyed. Here it happens to be social security; there in Haiti it was pigs. And in the 1990s it was rice farmers, so now Haiti cannot feed itself. Why? Because of Clinton's demands on Aristide's return....

P: *It seems to me, this is part of the western globalization agenda.*

C: Well, it is just an extension of Western imperialism. It goes all back; it takes different forms at different times, but fundamentally it's the same thing. I mean, take George Kennan, who just died yesterday. I was reading the obituaries today, but you're not going to read in the obituaries what he actually said. When he was in power, he was ... liberal icon. With regard to Latin America, he said that the U.S. should not hesitate before police repression by the governments because it is necessary to carry out police repression to bar the communists, like Haitian farmers, because we have to protect our resources, so therefore they have to have police states. I mean that is George Kennan; you know he's a liberal hero.

P: *Do you think that.... It could be poor Haitians, Somali or Salvadorians.., do you think that they can benefit from globalization to a certain extent?*

C: Globalization is a word we shouldn't even use. I mean globalization is a fine thing and everybody is in favor of it. The people who met at the world social forum at Porto Alegre...That is a perfect example of globalization. They are coming from all over the world; they are poor people, working people, *campesinos* (i.e., peasants)..., activists...that's globalization. Globalization just for the people! What the West calls globalization is a particular version of industrial investor rights integration, so globalization means neoliberal economic policies, which are not free-market policies. That is completely bullshit. They are highly protectionist in all sorts of ways, which many economists refuse to look at for ideological reasons, but it is a particular form of integration, which benefits investors and banks. I mean, o.k., we don't have to call that globalization. Globalization means just international integration, and there are forms – there would be a version of globalization which would be beneficial to people, but they are not going to consider it. It is the same with NAFTA. You know when NAFTA was instituted in 1994, the two major reports came out about NAFTA: one from the American Labor Movement, one from the Congress' Research Bureau, the Office of Technology Assessment–they all said pretty much the same thing. They said this version of NAFTA is going to be harmful to working people and farmers in all three countries, but it will be beneficial for investors. However, we're in favor of a different version of NAFTA, one which would be oriented towards high-growth, high-wages, equality, productivity, and so on, and they laid out details. So they were not opposed to NAFTA; they didn't want the executive version. The press refused to publish one single word about it. To this day, they have not reported it. Not even scholars report it because you're supposed to follow orders, and orders are globalization means what the rich guys want and not what the people and farmers in the three countries want. The population in all three countries… NAFTA is maybe the first international agreement in modern times, which was pretty much opposed strongly by the populations of all three countries, but 100% supported by elites, so you read the press except the population did not want it and for good reasons. It has done exactly what the labor movement and the Congress Research Bureau predicted: it has led to low-wage, low-growth economies for all three countries, just like they predicted, but a lot of profit.

P: *I'd like to shift from globalization to another topic that I am really interested in, that is, culture. As you know culture defines we are and we are not. It also shapes how we see the larger world. However, it seems to me when individuals are talking about imperialism, invasion/occupation, they seem to put more emphasis on the socio-political bodies and the material resources of the country being invaded than on its cultural and linguistic resources. As a linguist and critical thinker, how do you understand that?*

C: First of all, the imperial powers themselves are pretty conscious of it, so take the Indian classic case. The British instituted a system of education, which was designed to destroy Indian culture – they did not care about most Indians, they cared about the top 5-10%, more or less of wealthy elites. They wanted that they turn them into Englishmen, so they should get a class in English… education and become Anglophiles, pick up English manners so on and so forth, and they did! I mean to the extent, to an extent that I find shocking when I am there, you know. For example, the last time I was there, three years ago, I was in Calcutta, which happens to be run by the Communist party; West Bengal is run by the Communist. What they call the Communist party, it's kind of a European social democratic party–it is the Communist party in India with all the slogans…

Since we were guests of the government we got special treatment. One day they insisted that we go to the Victoria Museum. So, ok I went and we were guided around by the head of the Museum and 50 photojournalists taking pictures…It's a monument to British imperialism. When you walk towards it there is a big statue of Clive, you know the conqueror of India…You go inside – the place is lined with paintings, hideous 19th century paintings of British aristocrats beating Indians, who were lined at their feet… and finally you get Queen Victoria's tearoom. They managed to get her piano or something or other…. The point is that they were all treating this with veneration. I mean I would have thought that as soon as you got independence they would have burned the place down and that it is the same throughout the whole cultural system. I've got honorary degrees at places that are ludicrous, because they have all this pageantry and it goes back to the 17th century so on and so forth. They kind of laugh at it as they do it. Like, I once got one in Delhi… and it was worse than England, except they did not laugh at it because they had internalized the English values, which is very typical of colonial phenomenon. I mean the elite internalize the values of the colonial power; they sort of work for them. They are the ones who run the country and after the… you know… some revolution or liberation or whatever they usually often take up the same patterns. That is sort of what you're describing here [*here, Chomsky referred to the essay where Pierre talked about the effect of colonialism and neocolonialism on Third World countries*].

P: *Let's go back a little bit to, umm…*

C: But this is speaking of India–the educational system was geared towards West, so the upper professional class is sort of Western. It doesn't reach about 85% of the population. In fact, something like 85% of the population is literally in the black or informal autonomy, they don't even count it as statistics. There's a good study of it, but I mean like for example right now you read Thomas Friedman and all these guys they are just swooning about the marvelous, high-tech centers in … Bangalore... Which is great-they are better than MIT. On the other hand, right near them is the highest suicide rate in India that is going way up and the reason that it is going up because peasant farmers cannot survive neoliberal programs–the very same programs that are building the high-tech centers are also destroying hundreds of millions of people who cannot survive the import flow or they are being forced to agro-export. Instead of providing food, like Haiti, instead of providing food for the population, what you do is import stuff from big American agribusiness and you should grow export crops. The problem with export crops for one thing, they are capital-intensive. You want to grow cotton, specialized fruits and so on; you got to put a lot of capital into it. Furthermore, the prices are fluctuating all over the place. I mean you are a big agro-business and prices fall one year, you don't care. If you are a farmer and prices fall one year, your family starves to death. And that's what's happening. The other aspect of the neoliberal policies is that the government is supposed to leave people alone-which means they don't provide rural credit; which means you use usurers huge amounts of money. They don't develop irrigation; they don't provide the rural technical stations [as they used] to aid farmers.

P: *Speaking of farmers, it seems to me when people are talking about imperialism they don't seem to refer to issues related to land and geographical locations. To*

31

me, that is crucial. You cannot... one should not talk about imperialism without linking it to those two issues, so how do you...

C: The reason is that that involves just 90% of population and nobody cares about them, so why worry about it. I mean there are people who do, like this good work in India.

I mean what I was mentioning about India; a lot of studies by very good people-some of them British and some Indian. Actually one of the best journalists in the world, maybe the best journalist is an Indian journalist, who has done fantastic work on the Indian rural economy, but he does it by living with the people. So for the last 15 years, he actually lives with people in the villages, and when they migrate he migrates with them. He writes detailed, extensive studies of what is like to be the part of 80% of India and not the 10% that we hear about; so there is work. And they actually care about the land and the destruction of the land. One of the effects of high-tech agriculture, it is ecologically very destructive and that is going matter to people.

P: *Going back to Third World countries, such as Haiti, what role do you think intellectuals from the West and Third World countries should play or must play in the fight against social inequality, cultural invasion...*

C: The first they should do is to tell the truth. Instead of concealing everything that is going on they should let people know what is going on. If other people know what is going on in the rich countries, they are not going to tolerate it. If people in the U.S. knew the truth about what the U.S. government is doing in Haiti, they would never tolerate it. That is why it has to be concealed. And that's why they have to lie all the time. That is why you know you have to praise ourselves for magnificent effort in democracy enhancement because... after he tortured the people enough he sent in the Marines to restore Aristide on condition that he follow the platform of the defeated the U.S. candidate which was going to destroy Haiti. But that here is called a noble, humanitarian effort to bring democracy to Haiti, which then became a failed state because they have bad genes. All right, if intellectuals, if there were honest intellectuals, they would expose all this and the population would not tolerate it, and you have to change policy. And the same is true of Western intellectuals. And of course, there are some who do it. Take .... Jeff Sachs, they do it, but it's a scattering. Most intellectuals are servants of power.

P: *Given that...[interrupts]*

C: This goes way back. You know, I mean intellectual history is very distorted because... just think who writes it. Who writes intellectual history? Intellectuals, so they make it look pretty, but take a look at the real history and you find that 95% of them are....

P: *What is wrong with the world? Maybe I should ask, what is wrong with the imperial world?*

C: What's wrong with patriarchal families – If you have systems of power and domination, there is something that is going to be wrong. It doesn't matter whether it is a family or an international system. When you have concentration of power somewhere, it is going to be used to oppress people, almost inevitably. That's what's wrong. It is true of interpersonal relations and it's true of international relations.

P: *Do you think there should be a coalition between Western and Third World intellectuals in the fight against human oppression?*

C: If there are people like, say, Paul Farmer, yes. If there are people like 95% of the people at the Harvard faculty, no. It doesn't just have to do with intellectuals...I'd go to the...meetings...the international association...that's a perfectly fine interaction.

P: *Do you see any hope for the educational, political, and economic systems of Haiti?*

C: Look... I mean Haiti did something unbelievable in 1990. Haiti had an election in 1990 of a kind that is just unimaginable in the U.S. U.S. has never had such a free election, I mean in Haiti they did not elect–the choice wasn't between two spoiled, rich guys who went to Yale and joined the same secret society and can and have wealth and power because there are rich people fronting for them. In Haiti people were actually able to elect someone from their own choice. People had organized in the slums, in the hills, and had developed a real democratic society.

P: *So you're basically referring to Aristide when he was elected in 1990.*

C: The election in Haiti terrified the United States because it was a democratic election, and we don't tolerate that in the U.S. In the U.S., the population has to be excluded from the political process and sometimes it becomes just like a comic strip, like the last election, but it is the United States that is a failed state, not Haiti. So yes Haiti achieved something fantastic and that is why it had to be destroyed. As soon as that happened, it set off alarm bells in the United States. You know what happened.

P: *Given what has been happening in Haiti, what is the alternative- if there is any?*

C: What they did is an amazing achievement ...it's going to be harder now that the country has been devastated with war, but it is not impossible... And if it can be done in collaboration, it has to be done in cooperation with people in the rich countries. I mean, they are the ones who have the guns, and unless they can be brought into the solidarity movements, it is not much of... but with international solidarity, I think a lot can be done. And it is needed here too. I mean, look...unlike Haiti – it's a rich country, nevertheless; I mean it has gone through period of economic history in the last 25 years, which has no precedent. I mean for the last 25 years, for a majority of the population, the real wages have stagnated or declined and benefits have declined and people have to work harder and they are all in debt and so on. And it has got the worst health system in the industrial world. It is (i.e., the U.S.) not a disaster like Haiti because it is a far richer country, but structurally it is the same problem and that means there is a very good reason for cooperation, but that has to break through the doctrinal system, which doesn't let people know anything crucial. The more educated you are, the less you know ... so when you talk about these things in the Harvard faculty club...

P: *You are not talking about Haiti?*

C: No, here, in the U.S. the population simply doesn't know what's going on, and can't unless they do–either, unless they are in part of an activist organization which carry out research projects. But that can achieve something and it has in the past.

P: *...Before we adjourn...*

C: Anything you don't already know...[Chomsky smiles]

P: *Thank you.[Pierre smiles back]*

CHAPTER 4

EDUCATION UNDER OCCUPATION

Everything about human history is rooted in the earth, which has meant that we must think about habitation, but it has meant that people have planned to have more territory and therefore must do something about its indigenous residents. At some very basic level, imperialism means thinking about, settling on, controlling land that you do not possess, that is distant, that is lived on and owned by others. For all kinds of reasons it attracts some people and often involves untold misery for others.

Edward W. Said, Culture and Imperialism

Every act of conquest implies a conqueror and someone or something which is conquered. The conqueror imposes his objectives on the vanquished, and makes of them his possession. He imposes his own contours on the vanquished, who internalize this shape and become ambiguous beings 'housing' another. From the first, the act of conquest, which reduces persons to the status of things, is necrophilic.

Paulo Freire, Pedagogy of the Oppressed

Education may be defined as a process of continuous reconstruction of experience with the purpose of widening and deepening its social content, while, at the same time, the individual gains control of the methods involved.

John Dewey, Democracy and Education

As an educator, I have been interested in exploring the correlation between education and occupation for a long time. To my knowledge, not too many studies have thoroughly looked at how the occupation of restern countries by western imperialist powers has impacted the educational system of these countries. Studies have often scrupulously examined the socioeconomic and political effects of western occupation on restern lands. In critically reflecting on the dialectical relation between occupation and education, many pertinent questions have crossed my mind. I wish to begin this chapter by posing several of them: (1) How is it like to be in school while one's territorial spaces are occupied by foreign forces and/or by internal armed forces? (2) Can one possibly learn when one constantly has to worry about one's safety and move from one region to another to avoid bombs being dropped on one's house and one's head? (3) How can learning take place when these bombs destroy schools and other institutions? (4) Can one learn when one is constantly running away from bloodshed and terror? (5) Can learning be possible

35

when one does not know if one will wake up alive the next day? (6) Does it make any sense to talk about learning when one is facing hunger and starvation in an occupied land? (7) In short, is it conceivable to talk about education under occupation? As a "postcolonial" subject who was born, raised, and partially educated in a country that was colonized for over a century and later occupied for almost two decades, I have always wanted to seek answer to these questions. Hence, in this chapter I aim to explore these questions or, at least, cast some light on them. This chapter is divided in two parts: education under occupation and teaching under occupation. In the first part, I look at how western occupation of restern countries has drastically impacted the political, socioeconomic, cultural, and environmental structures of these countries. And in the second part, I examine how such an occupation has negatively affected the educational system of restern countries, thereby respectively the teaching practices and the learning of restern teachers and students. At the outset, I shall attempt to attribute a working definition to and critically analyze the word occupation. Such an analysis will be informed by historical events that have shaped the restern world from the 1900s to the present, including the U.S. invasion and occupation of Haiti, Puerto Rico, Panama, Nicaragua, Guatemala, and the Dominican Republic.

What is occupation? I would simply define it as the physical, military, and ideological settlements of a powerful country and/or group of people in a foreign land, which they forcibly invade and, thereafter, occupy it as if it is their territory. During the early stages of occupation, the occupying forces often use the media as a means to propagate lies and false hope about their violent act--because occupation is always done through violence--while instilling fear in the psyche of the occupied. During these stages, what helps sustain the occupiers is not so much the infrastructure of the country they occupy because such infrastructure is usually dismantled during the military operation that leads to the occupation. Rather, it is the ideological apparatus that they put in place in the occupied land before, during, and after they occupy it. The ideological apparatus is made of some segments in the army, agents of secret information, the church, and of course the media. Through such an apparatus, ideological agents of the occupying imperial forces try to manage to control the mind of the occupied people.

In most cases-if not in all-occupation of a foreign land is motivated by economic, political, and geo-territorial strategic interests of the powerful country that occupies it. However, these interests are always concealed by the occupying country, which often uses alibi of all sorts to justify its violent actions. Besides the harmful effect that occupation has on education, which I shall talk about in depth later in the chapter, it disastrously affects the environment, the culture, the subjectivity, thus the life of people living in the occupied land. By the environment, I am not only referring to the trees that are destroyed, the animals and the insects that are either killed or are fearful of being killed, but also to the water and air that are often contaminated as a result of the massive cluster bombs that are used during the occupation period. The debris of these bombs are often left abandoned on the ground and become as hazardous as the bombs themselves. Consequently, innocent uninformed children, who after the occupation continue to play on such ground as they have before the occupation, run the gravest risk of being infected by these debris and dying from them. This is the human tragedy that is not often reported by the western mainstream media.

The environment, which is smashed, not only constitutes the oxygen of living creatures, including human beings, but it might be to many people in the occupied land a spiritual force. Needless to say that, many of them might feel spiritually connected to it. Indeed, some of them might look at it as a source wherein the meaning of life lies. Thus, imagine how the occupied people feel when of all of a sudden foreign occupying forces squash the environment that surrounds them. Besides the environment, how about the culture of the people who are living under occupation? Does it stay intact, or is it severely affected by the effects of occupation? Here, culture is defined as a reservoir of aspirations, hope, and set of beliefs that constitute la raison d'être of a people and/or a community. Given occupying forces occupy other territories with an often agenda to "civilize" the conquered people living there, I would venture saying that the culture of the latter is inevitably impacted during occupation.

As a counter attack, the occupied people often use all forms of resistance, ranging from armed to spiritual resistance, to protect their culture. Such forms of resistance are in most cases the only option left to them, especially to those who do not want to knee and bow before the occupying forces. Their resistance is originated not only from their inner spiritual force but also from their deepest sense of human dignity and pride, autonomy, nationalism, and respect, which they try hard to preserve. For the occupied people, resistance is a human right that the occupying power cannot ever take away from them. The spirit of resistance gives them hope and strength to continuously and rigorously fight against the occupation of their land, mind, soul, and body by the occupiers.

The impact of occupation on the body of the occupied is an issue that has not hitherto been fully addressed. As I understand it, the body of the occupied is a very important concept that deserves to be meticulously explored in the context of occupation. It is via the use of the body of the occupied that the occupier humiliates the latter. The sexual assault that the occupied suffers from the occupier is a prime example. Sexual assault not only psychologically impacts the occupied but it also affects their human dignity.

Furthermore, the body of conquered people goes beyond their physical image. For example, it is through the use of the body of the occupied that the occupier culturally misrepresents them. It can then be argued that the body of the occupied people represents both their cultural and biological space, which should not be invaded and assaulted. Therefore, any attack against it, be it through rape, beatings, and cultural misrepresentation is a psychological blow to the personhood of occupied people. As for rape, which is very common during occupation, it is not merely a form of physical humiliation that the occupied, especially the female occupied experience, it is also a direct hit to their subjectivity, sense of self. Thus, it can be inferred from this analysis that like the mind and soul of occupied people, their body is worth taking into consideration when examining the multidimensional effects that occupation has on them.

To return to the cultural invasion act of the occupying forces that the occupied always faces during occupation, I would argue that it could be quite a challenge to counter attack such an invasion. The reason is that the western occupying forces always have at their disposal resources to control the media in the target land. Consequently, despite the resistance of the occupied people to western culture, such a culture eventually gets to invade their cultural and territorial space through institutional apparatus, such as schools and many mediums of communication, including the media. The media in particular is the tool by which occupying forces gain the consent of both their own people and those in the occupied lands, and which allows them to implement their politics of deceit and exploitation abroad.

Throughout history occupation has been the expansionist project of western imperial powers, starting with the Greek and Roman empires. It has been carried over by western countries, such as France, Great Britain, Spain, Portugal, and more recently the United States, which became an economic, military, and political powerful country, especially after the Second World War. Since the United States (U.S.) became an empire in the 1900s, it might have occupied more territories than any other imperial powers in the shortest period of time. Although sad and scary, its thirst to occupy lands that pose a threat to its interest is far from being satisfied.

It is worth mentioning in passing that it is not only western imperial powers that have invaded and occupied foreign lands. Non-western countries, such as China, Indonesia, Israel, and India have invaded and occupied countries, such as Tibet, East Timor, Palestine, and Pakistan, though their occupation of these territories is often supported by imperialist countries, such as the U.S. and Great Britain. As Chomsky and Herman (1979) note, "On December 7, 1975 Indonesian armed forces invaded the former Portuguese colony of East Timor, only a few hours after the departure of President Gerald Ford and Henry Kissinger from a visit to Jakarta" (p.130). Chomsky and Herman go on to assert, "The major point we wish to emphasize is that the United States and its allies are participants in the Timor massacres through the agency of the regime that they support in Jakarta" (p.131).

Occupation also takes place in other contexts besides the context in which an imperial power occupies a non-imperial country. Certain ethnic groups might occupy other ethic groups living in a different region though they might share same national territories. In this sense, occupation is like a form of control of a perceived weaker ethnic group by a "stronger" one. We have seen examples of this form of occupation in Liberia, Sierra Leone, Somalia, Rwanda, Sudan, and in Iraq where ethnic groups that are politically and military powerful have taken over and destroyed territorial spaces of those that are not as powerful. Regardless of the form and shape of any occupation and the economic and political interests that inform it, occupation is a violent act against the occupied people. Such a violent act, besides its devastating cultural, socioeconomic, and political effects, often causes a deep psychological wound to the occupied.

The long-term economic, political, and cultural ruinous consequences that result from western imperial powers' occupation of foreign lands have been explored through scholarly work of Noam Chomsky (1979, 1996, 1992, 2002), Walter Rodney (1972), Howard Zinn (2003), Edward Said (1978, 1993), Frantz Fanon (1963,

1965), Eqbal Ahmad (2001), and Michael Parenti (2004), among others. For example, Chomsky and Herman (1979) in *The Washington Connection and Third World Fascism* explain the extent to which western imperialist power like the United States has terrorized countries that they invaded and sometimes occupied. According to Chomsky and Herman, the United States has used the media as its servant to create a climate of terror and then invade countries, such as Vietnam and the Dominican Republic. In this regard, Chomsky and Herman (1979) note:

> During the Vietnam War, students were terrorists, and the government and mass media devoted great attention (and much outrage) to their frightful depredations (one person killed, many windows broken). The device was used effectively to discredit the antiwar movement as violence-prone and destructive-the motive, of course, for the infiltration of the movement by government provocateurs-and it helped to divert attention from the official violence that was far more extensive even on the home front, not to speak of Vietnam, the Dominican Republic, and elsewhere. (p. 6).

Similarly, Rodney (1972) in *How Europe Underdeveloped Africa* explicates how occupying European countries, such as France, Great Britain, Spain, and Portugal, dismantled the economic, political, and cultural structures of many African countries, such as Mozambique, Nigeria, and Kenya. Rodney argues these European occupying forces have destroyed the structure and infrastructure of the African continent through the confiscation and control of their land and the establishment of Christianity as a religious force to gain the consent and submissiveness of the occupied Africans. In the same vein, the legendary activist and historian, Howard Zinn (2001), brilliantly captures the devastating effect of Unites States' occupation of countries in the restern world, namely Haiti, the Dominican Republic, Nicaragua, and Guatemala. Zinn (2001) states:

> [The United States] sent five thousand marines to Nicaragua in 1926 to counter a revolution, and kept a force there for seven years. It intervened in the Dominican Republic for the fourth time in 1916 and kept troops there for eight years. It intervened for the second time in Haiti in 1915 and kept troops there for nineteen years. Between 1900 and 1933, the United States intervened in Cuba four times, in Nicaragua twice, in Panama six times, in Guatemala once, in Honduras seven times. By 1924 the finances of half of the twenty Latin American states were being directed to some extent by the United States. By 1935, over half of U.S. steel and cotton exports were being sold in Latin America. (p. 408).

The historical account of the occupation of restern countries by western empires that Chomsky & Herman, Rodney, and Zinn provide above is illuminating and very helpful. In fact, many scholars have often drawn upon their scholarly work to analyze further the negative effects of western occupation on occupied people. However, what I hope to add to their research is not so much a far-reaching historical inventory of the roots and motives of western occupation of restern lands. Rather, it is a critical analysis of its harmful effect on the educational system of

39

restern countries that have been occupied. Before going any further with such an analysis, I wish to state at the outset my philosophy of education.

Both as a student and an educator, my philosophy of education has evolved over the years. As a high school student, who was taught in a school system that mimicked and followed the rules and teaching codes of the colonial French model of education, I was taught to believe that knowledge is something that is transferred mechanically from teachers to pupils. As a high school student, I was not allowed to challenge and engage in a dialogue with my teachers and peers during class. I was expected to sit, listen, and copy what the teachers wrote on the board. Then, I had to study, memorize, and regurgitate back to my teachers what I "learned". Needless to point out that the teaching procedure involved rote behavior, and that most of my teachers failed to create space where I could use what I "learned" and linked it to real-life situations beyond the classroom's walls and the fences that encircled the school building. I was not encouraged either to make decisions on my own, to be creative and independent thinker, and problem solver. While there was ample room in my classrooms for plenty meaningless activities, there was little room for teachers' and students' interactions. As prime examples, I had to follow whatever my teachers assigned to me. My work was evaluated based on how well I followed what teachers did in class. I was mostly tested on what I was expected to copy in my notebooks even though my teacher's explanation was often unclear. I felt that poor thinking, writing, and reading skills that I acquired could only prepare me for routine and menial types of jobs in the real world. Freire (1970) in the *Pedagogy of the Oppressed* eloquently synthesizes this oppressive style of the education that I received. Freire summarizes it in these terms:

a) the teacher teaches and the students are taught;
b) the teachers knows everything and the students know nothing;
c) the teachers thinks and the students are taught about;
d) the teacher talks and the students listen-meekly;
e) the teacher disciplines and the students are disciplined;
f) the teacher chooses and enforces his choice, and the students comply;
g) the teacher acts and the students have the illusion of acting through the action of the teacher;
h) the teacher chooses the program content, and the students (who are not consulted) adapt to it;
i) the teacher confuses the authority of knowledge with his or her own professional authority, which she and he sets in opposition to the freedom of the students;
j) the teacher is the Subject of the learning process, while the pupils are mere objects. (p. 54).

Students who memorized and regurgitated to teachers what they "learned" via this rote teaching and learning mechanisms were considered the best students in my classes. At some point during my high school and college years, I was perceived like one of these students until I came across and read avidly a book called *Emile Ou de L'education* written by a French writer named Jean Jacques Rousseau.

Thanks to this book, I was finally able to draw the conclusion that the form of education that I was receiving from my teachers was not doing anything good to my young mind but domesticating it. The overarching argument Rousseau (1966) makes in *Emile Ou de L'education* is that pupils should be allowed to learn at their own pace and should not be expected to engage in any learning endeavor that is abstract and meaningless to their life. Education in this sense is conceived as a self-discovery learning process where pupils explore their learning without any forcible control of a teacher. Kneller (1964) captures Rousseau's philosophy of education and states:

> [Rousseau] stated that it was useless to expect a child to indulge abstract intellectual pursuits until he had reached the age of reason. Instead, a child should learn the things that he is capable of understanding through personal discovery. Followers of Rousseau urged teachers to connect what the child learned in school with what he would experience at home in his community, that is, to connect education and life. (pp. 104-105).

Although later in my learning curves I partially rejected Rousseau's view on education, at the time I found his radical philosophy of education refreshing and inspiring, especially after being mis-educated by almost all my high school and college teachers. I later refuted some of Rousseau's view on education because I felt and still feel that it is essentially a laissez-faire learning style that he consciously or unconsciously promoted through his book, which is worth reading nonetheless. Unlike Rousseau, I believe that if students are to learn, they need to be clearly guided and challenged by their teachers though there are people who manage to learn on their own. However, even the so-called self-learners do not construct knowledge alone. I believe they do so collectively with others, whether in school or in other settings.

As demonstrated above, before I got acquainted to the scholarly work of the Russian philosopher Bakhtin (1986), the American educator John Dewey (1997), and the Brazilian educator Paulo Freire (1970) who believe in co-construction of knowledge, my learning experience had already taught me that knowledge is constructed collectively. In other words, I already knew before being introduced to the work of these theorists that knowledge is not something that is automatically passed on from a teacher, who is believed to know everything, to a student, who does not know much or, worse yet, does not know anything.

Centuries before Bakhtin, Dewey, and Freire, Plato and Socrates already illustrated for us that knowledge is dialectically constructed through dialogue between teachers and students and mentors and mentees. Plato (1992) demonstrated in *the Republic* that through open dialogue, a mentee learns from his/her mentor and vice versa. The dialogue in which he and Socrates engaged in is a case in point. By creating space for a genuine dialogue between him and his mentee Plato, Socrates does not merely guide, teach, and challenge Plato, but he also learns from him. Although one might think that he is playing the role of a master, by dialoguing with his mentee, Plato, Socrates learns from him in the process. In my view, teachers' philosophy of education and teaching practices should reflect the dialogical

41

learning relationship that Socrates and Plato established between themselves as teacher and pupil. In other words, as Kneller (1964) puts it,

> The Socratic method is the ideal mode of education, since by it the student learns what he personally asserts to be true. The teacher-pupil relationship becomes intimate and personal. The teacher persuades the student to think by questioning him about his beliefs, by setting before him other beliefs and thus forcing him to probe the workings of his own mind. In this way the student accepts the truth, but only because it is true for him. (p.70).

My philosophy of education is grand yet simple. I believe that teachers first and foremost ought to be aware of what they are teaching students to become. In other words, before engaging in the act of teaching, they need to ask themselves questions, such as: Am I going to teach my students a set of fragmented knowledge and how to regurgitate it to people as tangible evidence that they are "smart" and prepared to meet certain academic, intellectual, and professional expectations, and fit certain social norms? Or am I going to help them develop critical thinking skills to dismantle this set of fragmented knowledge and reconstruct it based on their prior knowledge, lived experience, imagination, and own understanding of it? Am I going to encourage my students to take intelligent risks informed by their intellectual curiosity and personal interests? Or am I going to censure their learning by expecting them to open up their young mind and fill it up with a prepackaged information and knowledge that I prepare for and impose on them? Or am I going to encourage them to interrogate that information and knowledge and to figure out what piece of it they can relate to their interests and goals? Or am I going to single them out in my class for daring to question what I teach them and for disagreeing with my teaching approach and philosophy of education?

More importantly, am I am going to be willing to engage in a dialogue with them to find out more about their previous learning experience, different approach of teaching and philosophy of education, and be open to learn from them new ideas about learning and teaching? Or am I going to be continuously stuck in my comfort teaching zone expecting my students to passively receive and repeat like parrots the knowledge that I pass on to them? Or am I going to cultivate the intellectual and moral courage, the respect for human intelligence, and self awareness so I am prepared to treat my students as intellectual beings who have the innate ability to think critically, reflect actively, decide for themselves, and with whom I can deconstruct knowledge while, at the same time, constructing new ones in the process?

Teachers who are guided by a progressive philosophy of education are those who help students develop creative and critical thinking skills to continuously question their own learning, which should always be in the making. These teachers assume a responsible task to help their students understand that education is not how about many theories they "learn" through rote memorization. Rather, it is about challenging students to interrogate, constantly search, and figure out how these theories came into being; how they can relate them to their interest, intellectual needs, and life; and how they can use them to effect social change. Teachers who teach students to become critical and independent thinkers also take on a gigantic teaching task to help their students develop sociopolitical, cultural, and historical awareness/consciousness to challenge social norms, as opposed to prepare them to become mere docile adapters to these norms. Equally crucial, good educators are the ones who urge students to discover their own path through continuous search and exploration of novel ideas while providing them with genuine support and mentorship.

What students are expected to learn in school is meaningless to the extent they are not able to read their own meaning into it, that is, linking their own experience and interests to it. Students study and learn best when the relevance of what they study or are expected to learn is made clear to them or, better yet, when they themselves see its relevance to their intellectual interests, needs, or curiosity. Stated otherwise, something is meaningful to students so long they feel they can connect it to their own real-life situations and those of others.

Since their real-life situations might change as they go through many obstacles in life as well as higher stages in their academic and intellectual journey, students ought to be encouraged and helped by their teachers to cultivate intellectual flexibility and openness to try novel ideas, deconstruct prior ones, construct news ones, and take on new challenges. Their teachers ought to help them develop intellectual awareness, so that they understand that the knowledge they acquire, as a result of personal intellectual search and interaction with their teachers and peers, is not a fixed entity. Simply stated, they need to fully comprehend that knowledge is not like a beautiful piece of art they buy at an art studio, take it home, hang on the wall in their living room, and leave it there. Rather, knowledge is an intellectual acquisition, earned through struggles, that is, through social, cultural, and historical transactions with people and exposure to varying sources of literature. While knowledge should be highly appreciated and valued, it needs to be continuously expanded on, reexamined, questioned, and constantly put to tests.

As noted earlier, students should not be expected to develop all these critical skills on their own. They ought to receive assistance and guidance of their teachers. However, in order for all this to be a reality, educators need to make a conscious effort to reach out to and know their students, which can only be possible through genuine dialogical relationships. Knowing their students will enable educators to have a sound understanding of their learning styles, their cultural, linguistic, and historical repertoires, their prior knowledge, and how to help them build on that knowledge. Building on students' various repertoires and prior knowledge facilitates the learning process of students and the teaching practices of teachers and most importantly validates students' identities while strengthening their confidence and self-esteem.

Equally important, teachers have a professional and moral obligation to find ways to make the school curriculum accessible and meaningful to students whose backgrounds might not match with the content of such a curriculum. In other words, since education is the essence of life but not the means and the end to it, therefore in order for students to be able to relate what they learn in school to their lived experience, school materials should be based on real-life circumstances, rather than based on abstract theories and isolated study cases. To this end, it is critically important that students and teachers collectively question how school materials and curricular are selected and developed; what shapes them and where they come from. It is equally imperative that they interrogate which voices are being represented in these written curricular as occupied and colonized students' voices often are not represented in the learning materials they are required to use in class.

Since "the curriculum is often seen as the driving force for instructional practice, the framework within which day-to-day decisions are made" (Auerbach, 1985), should not school materials, such as textbooks, emerge from students' world and lived experience? If so, will not then such a student-driven curriculum, rather than an imposed curriculum allow much more space for students' active participation and interaction with teachers? As Auerbach (1985) maintained, when teachers "start from the students to the curriculum rather from the curriculum to the students"(p.16) students are able to arrive to construct their own knowledge and act upon it.

Drawing on Auerbach's contention above, it can be stated that in order to understand what fundamentally causes the mis-education of students, it is educationally vital that one looks closely at what is going on in the classroom in terms of how teachers teach, interact with, construct or fail to construct knowledge with students. I am not implying here that the mis-education of students should be placed on teachers' shoulders alone because such an argument will take off responsibilities of the school system, policy makers and the government, and overlook other factors, such as the negative effects of occupation on the school system, that might have contributed to it. However, teachers' teaching practices, proper and/or lack of proper training, their attitude towards, level of trust in students, and level of investment in the learning of each student need to be taken into consideration, for arguably these factors play a crucial role in students' academic achievement and/or lack of achievement.

As an educator, it took me a long time before I finally understood the vital role a culturally relevant and meaningful curriculum plays in student learning. It also took me a long time to understand how crucial it is to know first and foremost my students and use their prior knowledge as a building block in order to help them achieve academically. I come to that understanding through my personal schooling experience; the contact with the great works of Dewey (1997), Backtin (1986), Vygotsky (1978), and Freire (1970); the acquisition of various teaching methods and theories in multicultural education articulated by Nieto (1992) and Grant & Sleeter (1987); and through constant self-questioning on what kind of teacher I want to become and how I would teach my students to become what they want to be.

Before I became a teacher, after long introspection I questioned myself as to whether I had the human understanding and political and cultural awareness to teach effectively. I also wondered if I had a strong enough sense of social justice, responsibility, and commitment to begin this long journey. This was when the immensity of the teaching profession seemed really challenging to me, for I knew whatever I taught my students in the classroom would impact their lives. These puzzling questions were left unanswered until I started teaching ESL/Reading to immigrant students. Working with these students made me realize that I could not teach them these subjects without considering their cultural background and identity, which constitute an integral part of their learning process.

For the last five years or so, I have been teaching Reading and ESL (English as a second language) both at high school and college levels to students from different parts of the world. I know that what I teach has to matter to my students, therefore I have incorporated in my lesson plans thoughts and ideas generated from their classroom group discussions. Writing exercises and class discussions were usually generated from the questions that I have encouraged them to ask about their family, living conditions at home and in their neighborhood, and the socio-economic and political realities that they have to face in their daily lives. The concerns they express and questions they ask in class about these factors are part of the classroom experience. For example, my students are always eager to talk about their culture and experience as immigrants. Thus, to make what I teach in the classroom meaningful to them, I have produced a unit about culture and immigration. They write short essays in which they compare their culture with American culture and talk about their experience as immigrants living in the United States. Repeatedly, I have been amazed to see that all of my students actively engaged in the class discussion and activities. As a result of this experience, I have learned that teachers have an obligation to find ways to teach their students what is practical and relevant to their lives. From this experience, I have concluded that it is crucial that the school system has well trained educators who are capable of effectively teaching students the necessary skills needed to face the multiple challenges in the real world.

Teaching students of various ethnic, cultural, linguistic, and social class backgrounds has made me fully aware that students need full support and encouragement from their teachers to preserve their cultural heritage and identity. This might help them connect with the past, make sense of the present, and prepare them for future. While I was pursuing my undergraduate degree, I personally experienced the pain of being in a classroom where I deeply felt that my cultural and linguistic backgrounds were being attacked and devalued by some of my professors and classmates. I got to a point where I almost dropped out of college because I felt so alienated in the classroom. The message that I felt was being sent to me directly or indirectly from some of my peers and professors was that "if you are not like us, then you are an outsider." Thus, I had to use my inner force to overcome this sense of isolation so that I could complete my undergraduate degree.

Now reflecting back on this "savage" learning experience (Kozol, 1991) as an educator, I have come to the conclusion that teachers who are biased and lack political and cultural awareness can negatively affect students' self worth and the course of their learning based on how they perceive and treat them in their class. To simply put it, a teacher can psychologically and educationally break his or her students in small pieces. This painful experience, however, did not stop me from continuing to strongly believe that educators, especially those who believe in social justice, can play the role of agents of social change by helping their students develop a language of critique to question and actively participate in countering western occupation of their lands. Is it possible to find teachers within the school system of an occupied country to be willing to take on these multiple tasks mentioned above? It is to this question that I shall turn next.

TEACHING UNDER OCCUPATION

As mentioned earlier, the cultural, socioeconomic, and political systems of an occupied country are not the only components that get damaged during occupation. Equally damaging is the school system of the occupied country through which the occupying power circulates its lies and falsification about the history of occupied people. To achieve such a goal, the occupying force tries to control the school system by getting rid of teachers who pose a threat to its corporate interest and hiring new teachers who serve such an interest. In some occupied lands, such as Puerto Rico, the occupying forces bring in teachers from the occupying land to teach students in the occupied territory. They do so with a clear objective in mind, that is, to indoctrinate the occupied students by teaching them the language, cultural values, beliefs, and even the history of the occupying countries. Simply put, the conquering countries ensure that they have their teachers invade the school system of the conquered lands because part of their agenda is to "civilize" the conquered people by inculcating in their mind western values, culture, and language that the conquering forces believe are superior to those of the occupied people. I wonder how an occupying force can "civilize" an occupied people through occupation, which is nothing else but a violent action against the latter. In my view, occupation can only lead to the "de-civilization " of the occupied whose culture and language are belittled while their national sovereignty and citizenship are subject to assault during the occupation period. I shall expand in chapter six on the question of culture and language as far as colonized and occupied people in the restern world are concerned.

Joel Spring (2004) in his book, *Deculturalization and the Struggle for Equality*, provides us with a historical account of how the United States has attempted through school to "deculturalize" occupied people, such as Puerto Ricans and Native Americans. Spring argues that Native Americans' lands were not only confiscated by the white American dominant class in cahoots with the American government, but they were also forced to fully embrace through school white Anglo culture. They were forbidden to speak their languages and wear their traditional cloths. Moreover, at school, they were forced to speak, dress, and behave like the Anglos, or else they were severely punished.

Similarly, Spring goes on to point out that, four years after their country became an autonomous nation, Puerto Rican students were compelled to speak only English in school and embrace Americans' (of the United States) ways of life at the expense of their own. To ensure that English and American culture prevailed in the school system of this island, it was mandatory that teachers spoke only English in their classrooms as well as during meetings. Some of them were sent to the United States to be trained, i.e. mastering the English language and American's cultural values, customs, and beliefs, so that they can transmit those cultural norms to the conquered Puerto Rican students.

Spring (2004) recounted a few historical facts about U.S. commissioners of education in Puerto Rico. Paraphrasing Spring, these commissioners wanted to wipe out the language and culture of Puerto Rican students through the implementation of their school policies. With regard to the Puerto Rican school system, one of the U.S. commissioners of education, Brumbaugh, stated: "No school has done its duty unless it has impressed devout patriotism upon the hearts and minds of all the children" (In Spring, 2004). By this, Brumbaugh meant patriotism that Puerto Rican students needed to show in favor of the U.S. conquering empire. In fact, Puerto Rican students were compelled to pledge allegiance to the U.S. flag while they were taught American national songs and anthems and historical facts about American heroes. Capturing Brumbaugh's imposition of American cultural and historical values on Puerto Rican students, Spring (2004) notes:

> He recruited teachers from the United States. Most of these teachers spoke only English, which meant that by default their instruction was not bilingual. Every school on the island was given an American flag, with most of them being donated by the Lafayette Post, Army of the Republic, New York City. The raising of the U.S. flag was used to signal the commencement of classes. Patriotic exercises were organized in the school with children being taught U.S. national songs such as 'America,' 'Hail, Columbia,' and 'The Star-Spangled-Banner." (p. 92).

Similar to Spring's historical account, Aida Negron De Montilla (1971) explained in her book *Americanization in Puerto Rico and the Public-School System 1900-1930* the extent to which Americanization has been imposed on Puerto Rican Students through the school system that was structured and molded according to the U.S. educational agenda. De Montilla synthesized the ideological and cultural mechanisms that the U.S. conquering power put in place in the Puerto Rican school system to execute its imperial agenda. She pointed out these mechanisms through the following list:

a) Required celebration of U.S patriotic holidays, such as the fourth of July, which had not been celebrated prior to conquest.

b) Patriotic exercises designed to create allegiance to the United States, such as pledging allegiance to the U.S. flag and studying important historical figures of U.S. history.

c) Replacing local textbooks and curricular with ones reflecting the way of life in the United States.

d) Attempts to expel teachers and students who engaged in anti-U.S. activities.

e) Attempts to use teachers from the United States as opposed to local teachers.

f) Introduction of organizations, such as the Boy Scouts of America, to promote allegiance to the United States.

g) Attempts to replace Spanish with English with English as the language of instruction.

These facts about the United States' educational and cultural invasion in Puerto Rico that De Montilla nicely summarized above can also to a great extent be applied to other conquered U.S. lands, such as the U.S. Virgin islands and France occupied territories, such as Martinique and Guadeloupe. However, talking in detail about these conquered territories is beyond the scope of this chapter. Hence, I would add to Spring's and De Montilla's arguments, asserting that importing teachers from the metropolitan and instituting them within the school system of occupied lands has been the teaching and ideological practices that western colonial countries have throughout history used to defend their interests. These practices are still at work in this age of neoliberalism though they might be implemented somewhat differently, but the end result is the same.

I wish now to talk about the oppression that progressive teachers experience while teaching in a school system that is conquered by western occupying forces. This form of oppression sometimes entails the isolation and even assassination of these teachers who have historical consciousness, which empowers them to resist a western version of their own history. These teachers are subject to isolation and sometimes murder because potentially they could dangerously help the youth and other members of their society to discover the truth about their own history. History in this sense becomes a dangerous weapon that can be used to mobilize occupied people to revolt against all the lies they have been told. History can also be utilized as an ideological tool to render passive and desensitize an occupied people about sociohistorical, economic, and political conditions that have impacted their lives. This explains why the ideological and political struggle for liberating and/or oppressing people is usually revolved around and highly depends on whose version of history that prevails and gets registered in one's mind. Specifically, in the context of western occupation of restern lands, the ideological battle is centered around which historical facts that are being concealed to serve the interests of the occupying western forces. History is then located in the center of discussions of great educational, socioeconomic, and political importance as far as western occupation, colonization, and domination of the "other" are concerned.

Like servant teachers of western occupying powers, reactionary teachers through western neoliberal school systems often conceal historical facts from marginalized students. Moreover, many of these teachers teaching in the so-called modern, civilized, democratic, and free lands, engage in the falsification of historical facts to obtain the consent and passivity of students. Among these students who are lied to about their history, many of them sometimes end up naively accepting corporate practices of western empires. Teachers' retrograde and neoconservative views, manipulation, and/or covering up of world historical facts will be discussed in depth in the next chapter.

I wish to go on here, arguing that literary and geographical facts are as important as historical facts when one analyzes the attempt of occupying forces to control the school system of the occupied land. These facts play a major role in the educational growth of and are rooted in the cultural consciousness of students.

Broadly defined here, Literature is the subject and/or the field through which students acquire the information and knowledge about their culture and that of others; while Geography is the discipline that allows them to have a sense of how the world is strategically located and politically divided to serve the political, economic, and socio-cultural interests of certain countries at the expense of others'. Thus, having a clear understanding of geographical divisions and subdivisions of the word will enable students to question why certain territories are taken away from countries to which once these territories belonged. Such an understanding will also empower them to interrogate and probably unveil the hidden agenda of certain countries that invade and occupy the territory of other countries and settle in for decades. Moreover, having a sound historical understanding of Geography will empower students to conduct a critical analysis of the underlying reasons that led some countries to militarize and build fences by their borders to separate themselves from other countries.

Finally, just as World History, having a clear understanding of Geography and its importance in the world is a dangerous knowledge to allow occupied students to have. In other words, allowing these students who are living and learning under occupation to have access to a sound understanding of their own geography automatically constitutes an eminent menace to the interests of western occupying forces. This is the prime reason why once the occupying forces take over the occupied countries, they first try to change the structures of the school and political systems of these countries. They do so by forcibly replacing school materials that reflect the geographical, historical, social, cultural, and linguistic realities of occupied students by a canonical curriculum whose content serves only the ideological, cultural, political, and socio-economic interests of the occupying forces. In occupied countries, students are taught in school that the occupying forces take over their lands with the unique mission and goals to save them from tyranny and poverty to which their own government subjects them.

These students are often forced to learn the language and culture of the occupier, who is portrayed as the savior. Meanwhile, the government, (be it democratic like the governments of Salvador Allende in Chile in 1971 and Jacobo Albenz Guzman in Guatemala in 1954) which was in power before foreign invasion and then occupation, is overthrown, while political and social activists who resist the occupiers are portrayed as "communists" or bluntly as "terrorists". Charlemagne Peralte, the Haitian social and political militant who bravely fought against the American occupation and was later captured and publicly hung by American soldiers, is a case in point. As George Michel (1996) explicated, after Charlemagne was captured and tortured by the American soldiers, he was presented to the Haitian population as an agitator, a communist, or simply a vagabond who was against the so-called restoration of peace and the establishment of economic prosperity and political stability by the occupying American forces.

During the period of American occupation of Haiti, from 1915 to 1934 and beyond, there were lots of forbidden truths to which many Haitian students were deprived access. If it was not for brave and courageous teachers who dared to "teach to transgress" (hooks, 1994) by informing students that Charlemagne, for example, was not an evil dissenter as the occupying American forces portrayed him, perhaps they would have still trusted the negative image that the occupying American forces portrayed of him. Moreover, if it was not for the countering discourse that some "communist" teachers (because that is how these teachers were then identified and called) used to demystify the lies that the occupying forces circulated through the school system, Haitian students would not have known that Charlemagne Peralte was a fine human being and a great activist who simply committed the "terrorist" act to resist and fight against the occupation of a western empire.

Haitian students through school and the media were brainwashed to believe that during the U.S. occupation of Haiti, American forces created lots of jobs and improved the health and the educational systems of this country. They were also misled to believe that the U.S. occupying forces restored peace and security in Haiti that were affected by the civil war that took place before they invaded and occupied the island. However, what they were not told was that these same forces murdered thousands of poor peasants who revolted against the high level of poverty and the assassination of members of their family that the American occupation forces engendered and took part in. Nor were they informed that these occupying forces exploited the financial and natural resources of their country and, before they were forced to leave, they trained and instituted an army, which has been destabilizing the country through many coup d'état and has been serving their interests for decades ever since.

For many Haitian students, myself included, it took them years before they were finally able to unveil all the lies they were told about American occupation. History of course does not lie, but facts that generate from it can be ideologically manipulated and reconstructed to defend the interest of occupying forces and dominant groups in society. As Freire (1970) eloquently put it, "By means of manipulation, the dominant elites try to conform the masses to their objectives. And the greater the political immaturity of these people (rural and urban) the more easily the latter can be manipulated by those who do not wish to lose their power" (p.128). Freire goes on to propose a counter resisting strategy to manipulation. He states, "The antidote to manipulation lies in a critically conscious revolutionary organization, which will pose to the people as problems their position in the historical process, the national reality, and manipulation itself" (pp.129-130).

Given the climate of constant manipulation of historical facts, the occupying forces' control of the school system of the occupied land, and the persistent terror that often leads to transregional and transnational migrations of occupied people from one country or a region to another, is it possible for students under occupation to learn and receive a quality education? What about teachers? Can they teach their students critical thinking, consciousness, and awareness skills under these circumstances? In short, can they teach for social change?

I wish to begin by analyzing and casting some light on the first question. My argument is that learning takes place when enough space is created so students can negotiate and co-construct knowledge with their teachers and peers, and when they feel they can use that knowledge to identify, then solve or, at least, come up with some alternative solutions to real socioeconomic and political problems they face in their daily lives. Expecting students to stay focused to study and learn while they have to move from one region to another to protect themselves and their families from being killed is simply an illusion of how learning takes place. Even when their schools, their home, and their families are not directly affected by the terror and violence that paralyze their country as a result of western occupation, psychologically they are impacted by this violence and terror. Therefore, what kind of education can one realistically expect students who live under occupation to receive? After all, the minimum education that these occupied students receive from servant teachers of the occupying forces might only prepare them to fit in and reproduce what these occupying forces have done to their families, neighbors, and compatriots, unless they redefine who they are and come to the discovery of their true self in the process.

What about the handful of teachers who run the risk of teaching to challenge and change the status quo? They unquestionably have a colossal pedagogical task to assume in order to reach such a noble and heroic teaching goal. To this end, they need to be ideologically, strategically, and methodologically well prepared to confront and transcend the climate of surveillance that the occupying forces create through the school system so education for praxis and liberation would not take place wherein. Furthermore, these teachers have to be willing to take lots of risks if they are to succeed in that teaching path which is full of endless blockades and barriers.

Is it, therefore, worth engaging in such a struggle, which might not ever be ended so long the occupying forces are settled in the occupied land? Answers to this question will vary depending on one's philosophy of education and teaching. If one sees teaching as a way of securing a job while accepting the diktat to lie to students by telling them that the occupying forces of their lands are not the roots of their economic, social, cultural, and political problems, one would then convince oneself that it is a waste of one's time to be involved in such struggle. However, if one believes that the act of teaching is to educate, mobilize, stir up students' consciousness, and help them empower themselves by developing critical thinking skills to actively reflect on, act on, and transform socioeconomic, cultural, and political inequalities that trap and continue dehumanizing them, then one would assert that it is indeed worth engaging in and staying in that struggle till to the end. I would conclude this chapter asserting that any form of education that is not conducive to self liberation and liberation of others from socioeconomic, cultural, political, psychological, and sexual malaise that have long trapped them is, in my view, void of meaning. Making sure that students, be they students who are living under occupation, colonization, or in "free democratic lands", receive this form of education is a noble goal that progressive neocolonial, the so-called postcolonial educators, and allies should all strive to help them achieve.

CHAPTER 5

DE-WERSTERNIZE WORLD HISTORY

Towards an alternative understanding of world history through the oppressed voice

History and context are crucial for anti-colonial undertakings. Understanding our collective past is significant for pursuing political resistance.

George J. Sefa Dei, Anti-colonialism and Education

'History is the memory of states,' wrote Henry Kissinger in his first book, A World Restored, in which he proceeded to tell the history of nineteenth-century Europe from the viewpoint of the leaders of Austria and England, ignoring the Millions who suffered from those statesmen's policies. From his standpoint, the "peace' that Europe had before the French Revolution was "restored" by the diplomacy of a few national leaders. But for factory workers in England, farmers in France, colored people in Asia and Africa, women and children everywhere except in the upper classes, it was a world of conquest, violence, hunger, exploitation-a world not restored but disintegrate

Howard Zinn, People's history of the United States

The looking-glass school teaches us to suffer, not change it; to forget the past, not learn from it; to accept the future, not invent it.

Eduardo Galeano, Upside Down

History as a discipline should not be simply about past narratives. Nor should it be a discipline that allows students to merely hear about their past and move on. History should be a vehicle through which students question and "deconstruct" (Derida, 1976) the past and connect it to the present in order to impact future events. History has of course been taught in school. But whose history has it been? Has it been the history that reflects the reality of both the western and the restern world? Or has it been a history that glorified Napoleon Bonaparte and Christopher Columbus while rarely acknowledging the greatness of Toussaint Louverture and Simon Bolivar who, without sophisticated technology at their disposable, defeated the French and Spanish armies to set their people free from colonial subjugation and slavery? Drawing upon on historical events that shaped both the West and the Rest, I aim in this chapter to analyze World History with a different eye, the oppressed's eyes.

Given the social milieu where I grew, it took me decades to understand the dialectical relationship between the past, the present, and the future. A dialectical relationship which, in my view, constitutes the fundamental triangle of humanity. For adults in my social milieu, however, it seems that one of the components of the triangle, the past, was a painful thing to talk about. They seemed to have an easier time to talk about its other two parts, the present and the future. Were not they right? Is not it a waste of human investment and intellectual energy talking about the past, which is already gone? Is not it sorrowful referring to a past that is marked of imperialism, thus bloodshed, human degradation, exploitation, and misery? Is not it a self-torture to speak of one's past that might haunt one's spirit and remind one of the devastating effects of slavery, as Alex Haley brilliantly illustrated in *Roots*. Is not it too dangerous to the mind of the youth to allow them to be aware of the cruel brutality of human subjects that colonialism caused, as evidenced in the movie *The Battle of Alger*? Finally, is not Wane (2006) right when she asserts that, "The struggle to retrieve the past and survive the present is an arduous journey?"

Analyzing these questions in a very superficial way, one might agree with the adults in my neighborhood who subconsciously seemed to fear the past while embracing the present and the future. Furthermore, given that one cannot shape or reconstruct the past, it seems logical to forget about it and focus on the present and the future. However, what (1) sense would have the world made to one's mind if it had only entailed the happening of the present and the uncertainty of the future? Alluding to one of the themes, colonialism, which I shall elaborate on later in the chapter, I wonder how (2) would its legacy and impact on human subjects get registered in one's mind if there were no critical questioning of the past? Finally, how would one be informed of the role that women played in the fight against slavery and colonization if one did not have a clear understanding of the past? In this regard, Dei (2006) notes:

> For colonized peoples decolonization involves reclamation of the past, previously excluded in the history of the colonial and colonized nations. They must identify the colonial historical period from the perspectives of their places and their peoples. Knowledge of the past is also relevant in so far as we as people must use that knowledge 'responsibly'. (p. 1)

Therefore, as one can infer from Dei's argument, trying to discourage the oppressed from critically questioning the "pastness of the past," Eliot (1932) is historically and humanly harmful. However, this has been the ideological tool used by the dominant class to maintain the status quo. Edward Said (1993) noted, "How we formulate or represent the past shapes our understanding and views of the present." Said's idea is clearly understood and appropriated by the dominant class who has been trying to control the mind of the oppressed through public consent so that they will not interrogate the past. This dominant class also understands that allowing the oppressed to interrogate the past might enable them to understand their present situation and how it came into being. And of course it is too dangerous to let the oppressed discover the truth about their past. Such a discovery is too threatening to the interest of the oppressing class. This logical reasoning that I am engaging myself in, here, hopes to help the reader unveil the hidden agenda of the ideological game that the dominant class has played to control the mind of oppressed people. The logic behind this ideological game is that, I shall contend, once the mind of the oppressed is domesticated, they most likely will be unable to revolt against their present inhuman economic and social conditions, which might have resulted from past historical events.

Going back to pertinent issues such as slavery and colonization, I would argue that encouraging silence about these issues is not only humanly harmful but it is also intellectually irresponsible, as Said (1993) reminds us. Said states:

> ...One cannot postpone discussions of slavery, colonialism, racism in any serious investigations of modern Indian, African, Latin and North American, Arabic, Caribbean, and Commonwealth literature. Nor is it intellectually responsible to discuss them without referring to their embattled circumstances either in post-colonial societies or as marginalized and/or subjugated subjects confined to secondary spots in the curricula in metropolitan centers. (p.316).

Postponing discussions of important issues, such as slavery, colonialism, and racism, as Said mentioned above, has been the tireless ideological strategy that the white dominant class has used to stay in powerful positions in society. And institutions, such as school, the media, and church have been in some cases the channels through which outright lies and silence about these issues have been circulated. In other words, these institutions have been used as an ideological apparatus tool to freeze people's "presence of mind" (Leistyna, 1999) so that they can become docile recipient of the dominant class' lies, which are usually aimed to make the oppressed loyal and obedient servants of the imperial world.

It is no accident that history of colonialism and neocolonialism is rarely taught in most universities here in the U.S. It is not an accident either that post-colonial studies have not been funded at some universities in the U.S. However, disciplines such as engineering, business administration, and computer science, which generally do not question the status quo, have been greatly funded. It will be simply too dangerous to allow neocolonial subjects to have access to true historical facts that might empower them to stand against their long time oppressors. It will be even more dangerous to allow "this group of people," as they are often described by the dominant class, to find out that the true version of world history has been mostly confiscated by white western conservative dominant groups. The artificial version of world history that they have made available to neocolonized subjects has been written in a way that serves their interest. Had the oppressed group been allowed to know the truth about past events that shaped their lives, they would have certainly demanded world history to be rewritten in a way that is not biased, that is, in a way that recognizes and values the heroic action and powerful voices of Toussaint Louverture; Patrice Lumumba; Simon Bolivar; Amical Cabral; and Walter Rodney, among others, who have been somewhat silenced and put in a narrow historical box through the western version of world history written by the white dominant class. Furthermore, the oppressed would have been knowledgeably well prepared to refute "lies that they have been told in school by their teachers," as Loewen

(1994) pointed out, about Christopher Columbus, the so-called discoverer of the new world. They would also have wanted to know, as brilliantly captured by Howard Zinn, what "Columbus did to the Arawaks of the Bahamas, Cortes did to the Aztecs of Mexico, Pizarro to the Incas of Peru, and the English settlers of Virginia and Massachusetts to the Powhatans and the Pequots." Equally crucial, they would have wanted to have access to the truth about their own history, that is, history of their people, who were great scientists, philosophers, inventors, real warriors, and yet have been shadowed throughout the western version of world history. Finally, have the oppressed been taught the restern version of world history, they would have certainly known the following historical facts:

1. The Indians invented a nascent form of calculus centuries before Leibniz invented calculus in Europe (Joseph, 2001).
2. The Arabs coined the term algebra and invented decimal fractions: point twenty-five for one over four (Ibid. p.29).
3. The Indians developed the use of zero and negative numbers perhaps a thousand years before these concepts were accepted in Europe (Teresi, 2002 p.28).
4. The Mayans invented zero about the same time as the Indians, and practiced a math and astronomy far beyond that of medieval Europe (Ibid., p.13).
5. Native Americans built pyramids and other structures in the American Midwest larger than anything then in Europe (Teresi, 2002).
6. The Egyptians also developed the concept of the lowest common denominator, as well as a fraction table that modern scholars estimate required-eight thousand tedious calculations to compile (Hogben, 1942).
7. The Olmecs and Zapotes in Southern Mexico, the Maya in Southern Mexico, Guatemala, and Belize, and finally the Aztecs were founding civilizations before the Spaniards conquered Central America, murdered the native people, and exhausted their resources (Teresi, 2002).
8. Aristotle struggled to accept the fact that the Egyptians developed math before his countrymen. He argued: "The mathematical sciences originated in the neighborhood of Egypt because there the priestly class was allowed leisure" (Fowler, 1987).
9. The mathematical foundations of Western science is an intelligent gift from the Indians, Egyptians, Chinese, Arabs, Babylonians, and other" (Teresi, 2002).
10. Finally, in spite of the fact that we were told that Democritus was the first particle physicist, his idea was not a new idea (Teresi, 2002, 1999). According to Steven Weinberg (1992) "Indian metaphysicists came upon the idea of atoms centuries before Democritus" who drew upon the ideas of his predecessors to come up with many of ideas endorsed today by physicists.

The above historical facts make clear that history needs be retold in way that encompasses and captures the significant contributions of restern scientists and inventors to the scientific advancement of the world. Once the prohibited historical truth is told, restern scientists and inventors will no longer be denied full credit for their discovery and inventions. No longer will their legacy be shadowed in western history textbooks. My argument is that oppressed groups need to have access to the truth about restern scientists, inventors, and heroic historical figures who shaped world history.

As noted earlier, history has been taught al all levels in school from kindergarten to college levels. But from what and whose perspective has it been taught? Has not it been the history that reflects and protects the interest of the western world? Has the history of the neocolonial subjects and the oppressed been taught to them? If so, has it been taught by teachers emerging from the group of the neocolonized? Or alternatively, has it been taught by those who are knowledgeable and historically conscious and sensitive to neocolonial subjects' long historical struggle?

History should be a fountain of knowledge from which one can   retrieve varying historical features of the past. Such historical features of the fast should aim to empower oppressed people so they can make sense of what shapes their historical being, as well as what informs or should inform their present and future beings. In other words, history should be used as a tool to interrogate or better yet "deconstruct," (Derrida, 1976) the past in order to have a better understanding of it. In short, as Zinn notes:

> If history is to be creative, to anticipate a possible future without denying the past, it should, I believe, emphasize new possibilities by disclosing those hidden episodes of the past when, even if in brief flashes, people showed their ability to resist, to join together, occasionally to win. I am supposing, or perhaps only hoping, that our future may be found in the past's fugitive moments of compassion rather than in its solid centuries of warfare. (p. 11).

REVITALIZING AND HONORING THE PAST

Any society that genuinely cares for the intellectual nourishment and growth of the youth should strongly encourage them to critically analyze historical events that have shaped the past. This, I would argue, will help them become culturally and historically informed critical beings. Past events should not be frozen or buried in the past. Rather they should be revitalized, cherished, honored, and used to inform us what path to take in order to enlighten our present life with hope, whose power will enable us to shape or at least imagine a world of possibilities for everyone regardless of their racial, ethnic, linguistic, social class backgrounds, and sexual orientation. This is brilliantly captured by Trask (1991), who argues that, "we do not need, nor do we want to be liberated from our past because it is source of our understanding...We stand firmly in the present, with our back to the future, and our eyes fixed upon the past, seeking historical answers for present-day dilemmas" (from Dei, 2006). Unfortunately, standing in and blocking the path to a clear understanding of the past have been western colonialists and neocolonialists' ideological agenda. An agenda that reveals itself in their invested interest in preventing neocolonial subjects and oppressed groups from having access to a collective critical and accurate knowledge of their past. Western neocolonialists fear that if neo-colonial subjects and oppressed groups had a critical and sound understanding of their past they would then dare to imagine and fight for a better world, that is a world, where resources will be justly distributed between resterners and western-ers. Nonetheless, despite the ideological apparatus that has allowed western domi-nant groups to tell outright lies about the history of the world, some scholars emerging from oppressed groups in society have challenged those lies and insisted on finding out other versions of world history. They realize that if they fail to do so they will be just like Zombies deprived of recollection of who their ancestors and therefore who they are. Thus, it goes without saying that a critical analysis and understanding of the past is quintessential to one's historical being.

Historians and anthropologists, such as Cheikh Anta Diop (1991) and Walter Rodney (1972), are prime examples of scholars who refused to stay on the margin of world history. They urged their contemporaries and future generations not to live on the shadow of world history. In Cheikh Anta Diop's view, historical factor is of paramount importance. He believed that such a factor contributes to a sense of collectiveness and unity among people. Diop (1991) maintained, "The historical factor is the cultural cement that unifies the disparate elements of a people to make them into a whole, by the particular slant of the feeling of historical community lived by the totality of the collective." Like the activist Antiguan historian, Walter Rodney, Cheick Anta Diop tirelessly fought with his pen and brain against the dominant ideology of the European class that has strived to make oppressed groups become spectators of historical events. The scholarly work and intellectual activ-ism of this prominent Senegalese critical thinker have inspired many "post-colonial" subjects, including myself, to be actors/actresses and makers of history rather than passive historical events recipients. More importantly, Diop has en-couraged the oppressed not to miss the historical rendezvous to collectively and actively reflect on their past, act on their present, and envision a bright future for themselves and fellow human beings. This of course has made him and others be-come what I would call dangerous historical critical thinkers of the imperial world.

"These people," as the western conservative dominant class usually calls them, are fully aware that the past is such a great treasure to lose or to waste. Therefore, they have fought to keep it alive through critical political analysis and social activ-ism. They are cognizant of the fact that whoever has monopoly over the past will be in the best ideological position to invent and manipulate the law to control the disinherited. This is precisely the reason why these dangerous historical critical thinkers deem it imperative to interrogate the past and engage in an ideological battle with those who have been tirelessly trying to control it. They also understood that the propaganda that has been circulated through the mass media, schools, and churches to convince the marginalized to "get over" history of colonialism and slavery is a mechanism used by the western conservative dominant class to win the battle over the past.

It must be emphasized here that the battle over the hegemonic control of the past has always been between those who have been exploited and those who have been profiting from their exploitation. Therefore, it is not unusual to find privileged groups in society telling oppressed groups to move on with their lives and leave behind the sad historical past of their countries and people. Their convincing sounding slogan usually goes like this: This is the past; this happened years ago; we are in the 21st century; get over it young men or women; move on. This type of slogan is not neutral; nor is it innocent. In fact, I would argue that it aims to serve the interest of the western conservative dominant group which will always encourage the "subaltern" (Spivak, 1988) to be ignorant of their history, their past. The western conservative dominant class does not want the dominate group to understand that, "The starting-point of critical elaboration is the consciousness of what one really is, and is 'knowing thyself' as a product of the historical process to date, which has deposited in you an infinity of traces, without leaving an inventory. Therefore, it is imperative at the outset to compile such an inventory" (Gramsci, 1971).

This dominant group clearly understands that individuals who are able to critically assess and analyze their historical past can become a threat to its corporate interest. Therefore, these individuals must be kept ignorant of their history. This has been the political and ideological strategy used by the conservative dominant group in western capitalist countries. Though sad, this conservative dominant group has been thus far successful with this strategy. How has it been successful? How did this happen? My contention is that one can find answers to these questions by carefully studying the right ring dominant groups in society. In other words, one must study the right wings in order to know how they think, operate, and act. Otherwise, ideologically one will probably not be in the best position to strategically counter their hegemonic actions against oppressed people.

In ending this chapter, I want to emphasize that economic, social, and political dominations of the "other" by the oppressing group have been made possible by the latter's hegemonic control of the past. By maintaining oppressed groups in an ocean of lies circulated through western canonical texts and the mass corporate media, the oppressing group has been able to dictate what parts of world history to which the former is allowed to have access. The oppressed group thus far has been simply allowed to know "facts" about world history that would not threaten the status quo. Thus, unless history is rewritten in a way that reflects the voice of the enslaved, the neocolonized, and restern historical figures, the neocolonized and oppressed groups will merely be allowed to know the romantic version of their own history but not the true and real version of their historical past. As a result, this might lead them to narrate their story in a way that is not authentic, that is, in a way that merely reflects the western historical-dictatorship of truth. Fortunately, as previously noted, there have been historians and anthropologists, such as Walter Rodney, Cheick Anta Diop, and other ordinary people, who have challenged and resisted the historical dictatorship of western empires. They have done so by refusing to be simply observers of historical events that have shaped their lives and that of others. They have refused to be absents at the historical rendezvous, where the ideological battle over the monopoly of the past has been taking place. They want to be continuously there so that they can design or redesign current and past historical events based on their own understanding of the world history. We need to join them in the struggle to interrogate and rewrite world history through the lens of historical, socio-economic, and political realities of both the restern and the western world.

THE SUBALTERN LANGUAGE UNDER WESTERN SIEGE

Standard English is not the speech of exile. It is the language of conquest and domination; in the United States, it is the mask which hides the loss of so many tongues, all those sounds of diverse, native communities we will never hear, the speech of the Gullah, Yiddish, and so many other unremembered tongues

bell hooks

Because language mirrors social, economic, and political events, it is important barometer of a society at any given time.

Sonia Nieto

Colonial education has been one of the most damaging tools of imperialism because it has inculcated colonized populations from a young age with ways of understanding themselves as culturally worthless.

Mark V. Campbell

For many in countries with a history of colonialism, English literature texts have become considered not as timeless works of art remote from history but as complicit in the colonizing enterprise itself.

James McLeod

Many studies on language have focused on its syntactic and semantic structures. Over the last two decades or so other studies, such as postcolonial studies, have transcended this paradigm to propose alternative ways to look at language from an ideological, historical, and political standpoint. Aligning with this paradigmatic shift and some tenets of postcolonial theorists regarding the politics of language, I argue that language is not simply about uttering words. Language is intrinsically linked to ideology, culture, and power relations, as illustrated by Gramsci (1971) in *Prison Notebooks* and Foucault (1980) *in Language/Power*, among others. It is also the primary vehicle through which people stay connected with their identity and community and communicate their cultural heritage to the world. Equally important, as Nieto (1992) eloquently put it, "language is the lens through which one expresses one's view of the world."

Historically, a multitude of languages spoken in the world have been attacked and relegated to an inferior status through the mechanism of colonialism, slavery and an unequal balance in power relations. Consequently, people who by accident of birth happen to speak these languages have been marginalized, oppressed, and discriminated against. For example, in the United States Native Americans were beaten in residential schools for speaking their native languages that were perceived by the dominant class as "uncivilized" (Crawford, 1991). In Australia, Aboriginal children were forcibly taken from their family and placed in boarding schools where they were prohibited from speaking their native tongue (Olsen, 2003).

In South America, particularly in Peru, the Spaniards attempted unsuccessfully to completely wipe out the native language of the Andeans, Quechua (Pratt, 1999). Texts written in Quechua by the Indigenous Andeans took centuries before they were finally allowed to be published. A twelve-hundred-page letter written by an indigenous Andean, Felipe Guaman de Ayala, is a case in point. Written in 1613 and found by a Peruvian, Richard Pietschmann, his letter was not made available to the general public until 1912 (Pratt, 1999). Pratt maintains that, "Quechua was not thought of as a written language in 1908, nor Andean culture as a literate culture" (p.584). Similarly, it is worth noting that in other colonized or formerly colonized countries and states, such as Northern Ireland and Hawaii, people there have struggled daily to revive their languages, such as Gaelic and the Hawaiian languages. These languages have been under attack by colonizing and imperial powers, such as Great Britain and the United States. As for the linguistic oppression that Native Americans, the Tainos in the Caribbean (Crawford, 1991), and Latino/a students in the United States have experienced, it can be best articulated by what Freire (1970) called "cultural invasion" which, according to him, occurs:

> When the invaders penetrate the cultural context of another group, in disrespect of the latter's potentialities; they impose their own view of the world upon those they invade and inhibit the creativity of the invaded by curbing their expression. Whether urbane or harsh, cultural invasion is thus always an act of violence against the persons of the invaded culture, who lose their originality or face the threat of losing it. In cultural invasion (as in all the modalities of antidialogical action) the invaders are the authors of, and actors in, the process; those they invade are the objects. The invaders mold; those they invade are molded. The invaders choose; those they invade follow that choice-or are expected to follow it. The invaders act; those they invade have only the illusion of acting, through the action of the invaders. (p. 133).

Fortunately, throughout history the invaded have used their human agency to resist linguistic invasion by sticking to their cultural heritage and mother tongue in various settings, such as in school and at work, where they have been severely castigated for daring to do so. Gloria Anzaldua's (1991) linguistic schooling experience is a case in point. Anzaldua recounted her struggle with an Anglo teacher who prohibited her from speaking Spanish in class:

I remember being caught speaking Spanish at recess-that was good for three licks on the knuckles with a sharp ruler. I remember being sent to the corner of the classroom for "talking back" to the Anglo teacher when all I was trying to do was tell her how to pronounce my name. 'If you want to be American, speak 'American.' If you don't like it, go back to Mexico where you belong. (p. 203).

Anzaldua's experience with the Anglo teacher clearly illustrates how standardized languages like English can be used as an ideological instrument to commit "symbolic violence" (Bourdieu, 1999) against marginalized groups by silencing their voices. In the context of the U.S. school system, Anzaldua's experience shows the struggle of students whose home discourse does not fit into the mainstream discourse, as Cummins (1983), Nieto (1992), among others, has made evident through their scholarly work. Moreover, to paraphrase Delpit (1996) and Cope & Kalantzis (1993), her experience also substantiates the argument that students who do not have access to the code of power are more likely to be left behind in school.

The linguistic discrimination that Anzaldua faced in school might righteously lead one to question and challenge the belief that the United States is a free and democratic country. Specifically, one might contest such a belief arguing that in a country, which is called democratic and free, people should not be threatened and punished for speaking languages other than English. Prohibiting one from speaking one's language in a "democratic country" suggests that one is free in the land of the free as long as one does not speak Spanish, Chinese, or Creole, for English is the only language of freedom. Taking this analysis a step further, one might conclude that the hidden agenda of prohibiting people from speaking their own language is to promote English as the "lingua franca" (Phillipson, 1992). In this context, it can be argued that this type of linguistic assault against minority languages appears to have as its objective to put English into a class of its own. This, as a consequence, might dangerously "reinforce the dominant ideology, which presupposes that English is the most eligible language for virtually all significant purposes" (Phillipson, 1992, p.42).

As amply documented through research, this form of linguistic oppression mentioned above has often taken place in institutions, such as schools. During colonization, school was used as one of the major instruments to maintain the colonial power. In his seminal book, *How Europe Underdeveloped Africa,* Walter Rodney (1972) explains how that was made possible. According to Rodney, having control over the school system was one of the most effective strategies European colonialists used to domesticate the mind of the colonized Africans in order to perpetuate their practices of exploitation and subordination. To achieve this goal, they hired colonial servant teachers to mis-educate African students in kindergarten and primary schools. Through this domesticating form of education, African students were taught to simply become ignorant of their own history and geography, which these colonial teachers never talked about in class. While these students learned in school about the "Alps and the river Rhine" they were denied vital information about the "Atlas Mountains of North Africa or the river Zambezi" (Rodney, p.247). As early as in Kindergarten, they knew more about Napoleon Bonaparte, who reestablished slavery in Guadeloupe and attempted unsuccessfully to do the same in Haiti, than their own ancestors. Moreover, in this colonial school African students were taught to value the culture and the language of the oppressors but not theirs. As Rodney (1972) pointedly argues,

> Schools of kindergarten and primary level for Africans in Portuguese colonies were nothing but agencies for the spread of the Portuguese language. Most schools were controlled by the Catholic Church, as a reflection of the unity of church and state in fascist Portugal. In the little-known Spanish colony of Guinea (Rio Muni), the small amount of education given to Africans was based on eliminating the use of local languages by the pupils and on instilling in their hearts the holy fear of God. (p. 249).

As one can infer from Rodney's argument, the ideological agenda of the colonial school system was to ensure that the colonized did not have access to a sound understanding of their history and culture, which could have empowered them to revolt against their inhuman condition. Quite to the contrary, the colonized Africans were forced to learn the language of the colonizers for cultural assimilation and ideological brainwashing purposes. In other words, the colonized were compelled to gain certain level of French, Portuguese, Spanish, and English languages and culture, so that they could quickly assimilate into the European culture. Similar to the English Only movement in the United States supported by intellectuals such as Hirsch (1987) and Bloom (1987), this form of servile cultural assimilation during colonization was part of the agenda of the colonizers to maintain the status quo. The colonial form of education that was made available to African students was an instrument used to subjugate them while serving the corporate capitalist interest of the colonizers. As Rodney (1972) goes on to add, "Colonial schooling was education for subordination, exploitation, the creation of mental confusion, and the development of underdevelopment" (p.241).

What has been happening in the school system of neocolonized countries is not as prevalent as to what occurred in colonial school systems during colonization. However, it is undeniable that the educational legacy of colonialism continues impacting the school system of countries such as Haiti, India, and Tanzania. For example, in my native country Haiti, even after 200 years of independence, the language of the French colonizers is still valued over the Haitian native language, Creole. When I was in middle school and high school (from mid 1980's to early 1990's) all of the textbooks that I had to use for class were in French. Nowhere in these textbooks, either on the cover or inside, were there pictures that reflected the reality of Haiti. These textbooks were and perhaps still are a reflection of the cultural and historical realities of France, realities to which Haitian students like myself could not relate. As a result, a great number of Haitian students, including myself, felt linguistically and culturally homeless because there was no connection between what we read in these textbooks and our culture. In fact, as a high school student I always felt foreign and culturally and historically alienated reading stories in these textbooks, whose cultural and historical baggage was irrelevant to my lived experience. This is well captured by Kemph (2006), who eloquently argues that, "When students see neither themselves nor their histories reflected in their education, disengagement understandably follows" (p.132).

Like Kempf observes, not being able to see myself culturally and historically through school materials that my teacher used in class led me to resist what he taught in class. This also led me to question my Mathematics teacher's attitude towards the French language and culture. This teacher always took pride in recounting how well French educators trained him to become a Math teacher at a French Teachers Training Program in Haiti. At no time did he ever use in class a single word of Creole, the language I knew best as a working class student. Instead, he seemed to take pride in using French as the language of instruction.

Moreover, throughout my high school experience in Haiti, I was never encouraged by my teachers to challenge and try to deconstruct the hidden ideology embedded in the French textbooks that I was required to use in class. On the contrary, what I witnessed and personally experienced was that teachers were not only complacent about teaching French literature and history, but they also took pride in repeating, like parrots, to students their pre-fabricated knowledge about these subjects. At no time, did I recall my high school teachers attempting to question and challenge old French values, beliefs, and ideology entrenched in French textbooks that were imposed on them to use in class. Consequently, Haitian students, including myself, spent years from elementary to middle and high schools absorbing information that had no meaning to our lives. In fact, information acquired from these French textbooks structured my mind, to a great extent, to accept passively and reproduce the false idea that France is Haiti's mother country and source of knowledge.

After years of indoctrination, I became a docile reproducer of French values, beliefs, and cultural norms. For instance, until I developed critical consciousness, I used to believe that the French language and literature were better than Creole and the Haitian literature. As a result, through social interaction I always used French, the language of the colonizer, to communicate with and impress people, rather than Creole, my native tongue. What I was not aware of, then, as Wane (2006) notes, was that:

> The use of a foreign language as a medium of education makes a child foreign within her or his own culture, environment, etc. This creates a colonial alienation. What is worse, the neocolonized subject is made to see the world and where she or he stands in it as seen, and defined by or reflected in the culture of the language of imposition. This is made worse when the neocolonized subject is exposed to images of her or his world mirrored in the written language of her or his colonizer, where the natives' language, cultures, history, or people are associated with low status, slow intelligence, and barbarism. (p. 100).

Wane's remark speaks directly to my schooling experience in Haiti. Reflecting on that experience, I have come to understand that teachers or students, who lack historical and cultural consciousness, sometimes let themselves get trapped in the linguistic oppression of the colonizers, who always expect the colonized to speak the colonial language at the expense of their own. This sad experience with my Math teacher, more importantly, helped me better understand that the school system of a country constitutes its ideological apparatus. Therefore, if any radical social, cultural, and political changes are to occur, it must begin in the school system that has been historically used to maintain and/or challenge the status quo. It goes without saying that the school system can be a dangerous institution that reproduces the dominant ideology and/or a site of struggle where ideological and political fights for a just and democratic society can take place.

Furthermore, looking back at my schooling experience in Haiti, I now realize how sad it is that most of my high school classmates were more knowledgeable about French literature and history than they were about Haitian literature and culture. This is precisely what happened to colonized people during colonization. The colonized was more knowledgeable about the culture and history of the colonizer than their own. However, this did not happen in a vacuum, as Kincheloe and Semalia (1999) made clear in their book, *What is Indigenous Knowledge? Voices from the Academy*. Kincheloe and Semalia maintain that the colonized, through schooling, were taught that their indigenous knowledge was barbarous, uncivilized, and therefore was worthless in comparison to the European-based knowledge and formation they were receiving in school.

Linking Kincheloe and Semalia's argument to the Haitian school system that I knew as a high school student, I would argue that it was set up in a way that failed Haitian students both culturally and historically. In other words, this school system graduated students who might not have had a clear sense of their history and culture. Hence, locating this form of mis-education that my classmates and I experienced in a global educational context, one might ask: what can be expected of a generation that does not to have a sound understanding of its own history and culture? One might go further asking, what should educators do to ensure that the school system of their countries is not a duplicate of the old colonial school system and/or the western neoliberal educational policies?

Gandhi (1997) and Nyerere (1968) understood the educational significance and implications of these questions. Through their political career they attempted to address them in their fight against linguistic and cultural influences of colonialism on the school system of their respective countries, India and Tanzania. For example, Gandhi particularly advocated and fought for an educational system that met the linguistic needs and reflected the values, beliefs, and aspirations of the Indian people. While Gandhi did not object to the idea that students should learn the English language, he argued that the Indian indigenous language(s) should be valued and instituted in schools. Gandhi (1997) was disheartened by and therefore spoke against the dominance of English through public and private institutions in the Indian society. He maintained:

> Is it not a sad commentary that we should have to speak of Home Rule in a foreign language? Is it not as sad thing that, if I want to go to a court of justice, I must employ the English language as a medium; that when I become a barrister, I may not speak my mother-tongue, and that someone else should have to translate to me from my language? Is it not absurd? (pp. 103-104).

Gandhi's argument illustrates a very important point, that is, one's native language should not be ever sacrificed under any circumstance whatsoever. It is through that language that one can feel, breathe, and express one's aspirations and view of the world. Simply stated, one's native language is the language through which one can truly feel at ease in the world.

Similarly, Nyerere (1968) stood up against the educational system in Tanzania that was designed to prepare students to continue serving the interest of the British colonizers. To this end, he advocated for a more just and equitable educational system that would prepare Tanzanians to serve the interest of their country. As he pointed out, "The education provided by Tanzania for the students of Tanzania must serve the purposes of Tanzania. It must encourage the growth of the socialist values we aspire to" (p.32). Nyerere warned us of the danger facing a nation where the educated, upon completion of their academic degree, do not aspire to anything other than living a luxurious life, abandoning the rural areas where they grew up. He went on to maintain that when a nation has a group of educated people with such a mentality, the gap between the rural realities and the urban realities widens. This, according to him, happens because the educated usually tend not to return to rural areas to help and learn from farmers and peasants who might be knowledgeable in their own right but do not have access to formal schooling. Referring to Tanzanian peasants and farmers, Nyerere (1968) argued that their "non-scientific and academic knowledge should be valued, integrated, and indeed implemented in the school system" (p.13). Nyerere (1968) acknowledged the value of the type of knowledge that these peasants and farmers acquired through informal education. As he stated:

> The fact that pre-colonial Africa did not have 'schools'-except for short periods of initiation in some tribes-did not mean that the children were not educated. They learned by living and doing. In the homes and on the farms they were taught the skills of the society, and the behavior expected of its members. (p. 35).

Nyerere's argument addresses three key points: First, all kinds of knowledge have a certain value and can therefore be useful. Second, people are entitled to a quality education that prepares them to be involved in and serving their own community. And third, in the context of formerly colonized countries, individuals who have access to formal education need to work tirelessly to close the gap between the educated and uneducated by teaching and learning from marginalized farmers who have been deprived basic literacy. Nyerere urged the educated to reject the practice of the colonizers who created a division between the elite group and the uneducated poor. He believed that this practice would simply serve to maintain the status quo.

In this sense, the scholarly work of the late critical Brazilian educator Paulo Freire (1970) is somewhat similar to Nyerere's work. Challenging the traditional and oppressive forms of education, which he defined as a banking form of education, Freire advocated for novel and transformative ways to teach. He urged educators to draw upon students' lived experience and aspirations to teach them what matters to their life. Freire believed that teachers make this possible by creating space for genuine dialogue between themselves and their students. According to Freire, dialogue and critical reflection enable both teachers and students to understand, both at a micro and macro levels, socio-economic and political problems that they face in their daily lives. Such an understanding, in Freire's account, will in turn empower them to take action against oppressive practices that silence their voices, assault their human dignity, and deny them their human rights.

A Freirian educational approach is necessary and indeed urgently needed to understand how the colonial and neocolonial educational practices work and continuously impact the mind of neocolonial subjects. I use the phrase neocolonial subjects because people in the Caribbean, Africa, and in Latin America are yet to be linguistically and politically free and independent. For instance, in countries such as Martinique, as Fanon (1959) illustrated in *Black Skin White Mask*, people are still under the subjugation of French "linguistic imperialism" (Phillipson, 1992). Like the educated middle class Haitians, Fanon argued that the middle class Martiniquese, especially those who were educated in France, took pride in speaking French to interact with friends, family, and colleagues. However, they were ridiculed for speaking Creole to communicate their thoughts, aspirations, and feelings in public sphere. Fanon explained this form of linguistic self-internalizing oppression in the following terms, "The middle class in the Antilles never speak Creole except to their servants. In school the children of Martinique are taught to scorn the dialect. One avoids Creolisms. Some families completely forbid the use of Creole, and mothers ridicule their children for speaking it" (p.20).

Given this persistent linguistic self-alienation, one might wonder, what is the alternative? In other words, how is it possible to overturn such a linguistic colonialism and neocolonialism that continue to impact the mind of neocolonial subjects? To this end, McLeod (2001) suggests:

> Overturning colonialism is not just about handing land back to its disposed peoples, returning power to those who were once ruled by empire. It is also a process of overturning the dominant ways of seeing the world, and representing reality in ways which do not replicate colonialist values. (p. 22).

Drawing on McLeod's standpoint, I would argue that a plausible solution to the internalized oppression neocolonial subjects have experienced would entail the decolonization of their mind (Ngugi, 1986). How would this be done? Evidently, there is not a universal or a fixed answer to such a question. However, I would maintain that such a plausible answer can be found through what Freire proposed, that is, engaging in a dialogue with others and critically reflecting on and analyzing linguistic, political, and social problems that colonialism caused. The challenge, however, is that it is not only the mind of neocolonial subjects that need to be decolonized but also the imposed languages of the colonizers that they daily use. As Salman Rushdie (1982), suggests: "The language, like so much else in the colonies, needs to be decolonized, to be remade in other images, if those of us who use it from positions outside Anglo-Saxon culture are to be more than artistic Uncle Toms" (Rushdie, cited in McLeod). Along those lines, McLeod (2001) proposes that, "in order to challenge the colonial order of things, some of us may need to re-examine our received assumptions of what we have been taught as 'natural' or 'true'." Being able to do what both Rushdie and McLeod suggest, will evidently require what Freire (1970) called "conscientizao," which is individuals' awareness of linguistic, socio-economic, and political oppressions or, for that matter, any other form of oppression to which they have been subjected.

Linguistic oppression alongside other forms of oppression, in my view, are perpetuated through teachers' biases, ideology, and western colonial values embedded in texts that these teachers are expected to use in schools. Specifically, these oppressions get reproduced through the way teachers use and analyze these texts with their students. In this regard, Luke (1996) notes: "For human subjects, texts are not just something that they, as 'child,' 'student,' and 'parent,' use as part of a stabilized or fixed role or identity; these texts are the actual media and instances through which their socially constructed and contested identity, or subjectivity, is made and remade" (p.14). Thus, depending on how teachers approach and analyze texts, their teaching practices can empower students to reproduce and/or contest values embedded in those texts. Canagarajah (1993) for example, recounted his experience using Anglo textbooks to teach English to 22 students coming from poorly educated rural families in Sri Lanka, whose primary language is Tamil. The key textbook selected for the freshman English course was American Kernel Lessons. According to Canagarajah (1993), textbooks used in the school were donated by Western cultural agencies. Students enrolled in the English course were required to pass a mandatory English placement test in order to enter University. Canagarajah reported that the content of these textbooks reflected the reality of white middle class Americans to which his Sri Lankan students could not relate. However, Canagarajah managed to help students develop a counter discourse to strategically resist these western hegemonic texts. Canagarajah explains his students' strategic approach and resistance to these texts in the following terms:

> Through these counter-discourses, students could be detaching themselves from the discourses inscribed in the textbook and preserving themselves from ideological reproduction. Furthermore, students are able to construct for themselves more favorable subjectivities and identities through their counter-discourses. While the discourses of the textbook put students at a disadvantage, making them appear alien, incompetent, inferior and powerless, students' own discourses provide them confidence, familiarity, respectability and greater power in their social milieu. (p.151).

TEXTS, LANGUAGE, CULTURE, AND WESTERN NEOLIBERAL STATE

Willett et al. (1998) argue that, "a concern raised by language theorists and practitioners has been how to better understand and appreciate the significance of language in the production of power relations" (p.3). In the same vein, illustrating the pervasive presence and important role of language in ideology, Fairclough (1997) maintains that, "a critical analysis of language is crucial for social change." The argument of these critical theorists, particularly that of Fairclough, illustrates how language works and is used in the political body of society to empower and/or disempower people. Stated differently, such an understanding of the ideological and political aspects of language could empower marginalized groups to demystify the hidden ideology embedded in texts, such as political speeches and stereotypical messages circulated through the corporate media. Equally important, their ability to read what is hidden in language can help them unveil what is behind the action taken by the dominant class to silence languages, such as Spanish, Quechua, and Creole. In this regard, Dei (2006) notes:

> Language is a powerful tool for decolonization. The power to name issues for what they are demonstrates an ability to use language as resistance, and to claim cultural and political capital that is necessary to challenge domination. The power of anti-colonial thinking lies in its ability to name the domination and imposition of colonial relations. Language can be used to challenge the negations, omissions and devaluations of a peoples' social reality, experience and history. (p.11).

Similarly, Gramsci (1971) brilliantly capture "the significance of language in the production of power relations" (Willett et al. 1998) when he maintained that,

> Each time in one way or another, the question of language comes to the fore, that signifies that a series of other problems is about to emerge, the formation and enlarging of the ruling class, the necessity to establish more "intimate" and sure relations between the ruling groups and the national. (p. 22).

What Gramsci argues through this passage above unveils the unequal power relations between subaltern groups that have had to struggle in order to maintain and speak their languages and the dominant group that has tirelessly tried to make dominant languages such as English officially the lingua franca. Despite their resistance to the linguistic domination of the ruling class, minority groups have experienced some losses. For example, many bilingual programs, which have allowed linguistically and culturally diverse students to draw on the resources of their first language to acquire knowledge in and learn their second language, have been closed in some states in the US, such as in California and Massachusetts.

Given the above, I would argue that in order for "the subaltern" (Spivak, 1988) to continue to counter the linguistic domination of the dominant group, it is critically important that they develop critical consciousness or what Bartolome (1994) calls "political clarity." Such a clarity, in my view, will serve the following purposes: (1) It will help the subaltern group better understand that, for example, being forced to speak the so-called language of opportunity, English, at the expense of their first language is a convincing evidence of the dominant class's linguistic domination strategies; (2) the subaltern will also be aware that by forcibly embracing the language of the dominant class, they will automatically embrace values, beliefs, and norms embedded in that language; and (3) that once these cultural elements are engrained in their linguistic patterns and human consciousness, it then will be easier for the dominant class to manipulate and control their minds.

Fanon (1967) understood the implications of possessing a language when he warned us: "A man who has a language consequently possesses the world expressed and implied by that language" (p.18). Situating Fanon's argument in the U.S. context, it can be argued that once minority students, through ideological consent, are convinced to value and embrace the English language at the expense of their own, the cultural world of their oppressor to a great extent will become theirs. As a consequence, they might face the danger of consciously and unconsciously performing publicly and/or privately the dominant class' cultural values and norms through social interactions. As Ngugi (1986) reminds us: "Language carries culture, and culture carries, particularly through orature and literature, the entire body of values by which we come to perceive ourselves and our place in the world" (p.16).

Synthesizing Ngugi's argument, I would contend that if one wants to save his/her language, one should first maintain and protect his/her culture, which is the main branch of which language is an essential part. Linked to this argument is Amilcar Cabral's (1973) stance on culture. The Guinean and Cape Verdean leader, who fought rigorously against the Portuguese colonizers' cultural invasion in Cape Verde and Guinea Bissau, strongly urged people to heighten and defend their culture. Cabral dedicated most of his militant, political, and scholarly life defending the culture of his country both nationally and internationally against foreign cultural invasion. In his classic book, *Return to the Source*, Cabral strongly encouraged us to strive to preserve our culture from the colonial and imperial influence of the West. Cabral used culture as a tool of resistance to foreign subjugation of colonized lands, such as Cape Verde and Guinea Bissau. Cabral did not merely acknowledge the vital role of culture in the liberation movement. He emphasized and advocated for its full integration in the historical and political life of these colonized society at the time. He did so because he understood that imperialist and colonial dominations of colonized subjects also entails the cultural domination of the latter. Thus, Cabral strove to help his people be aware of the importance of using their cultural resources and values as a counter weapon in their fight against imperial and colonial powers. Cabral (1973) maintained:

> It is understood that imperialist domination, by denying the historical development of the dominated people, necessarily also denies their cultural development. It is also understood why imperialist domination, like all other foreign domination, for its own security, requires cultural oppression and the attempt at direct or indirect liquidation of the essential elements of the culture of the dominated people. (p. 55).

Drawing on Cabral's view on the political and historical importance of culture, it can be stated that culture is a vital tool that foreign invaders should not be allowed to influence, especially when a people engage in the struggle for self affirmation, determination, and linguistic liberation. The reason being, if colonized or minority people's culture is under siege, this might weaken their resistance to linguistic and political dominations of the dominant class. Defense and preservation of one's culture is key to one's linguistic independence, autonomy, and respect, regardless of what conservative intellectuals have argued.

One of the arguments that conservative intellectuals, such as Hirsch (1987), have articulated to impose English on linguistically and culturally diverse groups is that speaking one language will strengthen and unify the nation. Taken at face value, such an argument might convince one to believe that unity among people can only be achieved through one dominant officially recognized and established language like English but not through a plurality and diversity of languages. Hirsch believes that unity among culturally and linguistically diverse groups can only be achieved through what he called "common culture."

With regard to the achievement gap existing between underprivileged and privileged students, Hirsh (1987) argues that this gap stems from student's lack of a particular and prescribed set of cultural knowledge, which, according to him, can be learned through direct instruction. However, Kamberelis and Dimitriadis (2005) note that, "The cultural knowledge that Hirsh has in mind is presumed to be 'common culture' and not elite culture, even though it derives primarily from canonical works within a white, European-American, middle-upper-class, heterosexist tradition" (p.30). Similarly, Bhabha (1994), demystifying and challenging the hidden ideology and agenda behind the "common culture," states:

> Like all the myths of the nation's "unity," the common culture is a profoundly conflicted ideological strategy. It is a declaration of democratic faith in a plural, diverse society and, at the same time, a defense against the real, subversive demands that the articulation of cultural difference- the empowering of minorities- makes upon democratic pluralism. (p. 24).

What Hirsch fails to understand is that individuals do not give up their native tongue even when they are forced to embrace the "common culture" and assimilate into the mainstream. The reason is that one's language shapes one's subjectivity and sense of self. Thus, needless to say, attacking one's language is a direct attack to one's culture and identity. As Anzaldua (1991) puts it:

> If you want to really hurt me, talk badly about my language. Ethnic identity is twin skin to linguistic identity-I am my language. Until I can take pride in my language, I cannot take pride in myself. Until I can accept as legitimate Chicano Texas Spanish, Tex-Mex and all the other languages I speak, I cannot accept the legitimacy of myself. (p. 473).

Anzaldua's stance for her language and identity clearly indicates that language "plays a major role in the construction of human subjectivities and reflects their life histories and lived experiences" (Freire & Macedo, 1987). Her stance, most importantly, illustrates that, "Like desire, language disrupts, refuses to be contained within boundaries. It speaks itself against our will, in words and thoughts that intrude, even violate the most private spaces of mind and body" (hooks, 1994).

Linked to this is Villegas' (1988) description of how some Hispanic students insisted on speaking their mother-native tongue in spite of the fact some Anglo teachers prohibited them from doing so. Villegas states that speaking Spanish was repressed and fought against in school by some white middle class teachers who wanted their Latino/a students to believe this was in their best interest. She argues that these teachers felt that speaking Spanish in school was a way of persisting in being foreign. She goes on to say that although 90% of the students were U.S. citizens, their teachers treated them as outsiders because they persisted in speaking Spanish.

My contention is that such a devaluation of minority languages, as Villegas' research findings show, confirms that the U.S. school system is structured in a way that linguistically and culturally discriminates against minority students. Attack against languages other than English or French is not innocent. In my view, it is informed by the ideological agenda of dominant groups who, throughout history, have tried to impose their languages on marginalized groups as if the languages of these groups are not valid. Given the ideological battle revolving around language, is it not imperative that language be studied and analyzed alongside what is intertwined with it, that is hegemony, colonialism, racism, and social class? Gramsci (1971) defines hegemony as "the entanglements between the forces of political power, cultural ideology, and pedagogy which result in the domination of subordinated groups." Giroux (1992) elaborating further on Gramsci's theory of hegemony states:

> Hegemony refers to a form of ideological control in which dominant beliefs, values, and social practices are produced and distributed throughout a whole range of institutions, such as schools, the family, mass media, and trade unions... The complexity of the hegemonic control is an important point to stress, for it refers not only to those isolate meanings and ideas that the dominant [culture] imposes on others, but also those lived experiences that make up the texture and rhythm of daily life. (p. 94).

While Giroux clarifies the ideological and controlling roles that hegemony plays in the shape and structure of institutions, such as schools, family, mass media, and trade unions, Freire and Macedo (1987) point out the asymmetrical power relations and linguistic injustice lie in the English only movement:

> The English only movement in the United States ... points to a xenophobic culture that blindly negates the pluralistic nature of U.S. \society and falsifies the empirical evidence in support of bilingual education, as has been amply documented. These educators, including the present secretary of Education, William Bennet, fail to understand that it is through multiple discourses that students generate meaning in their everyday social context. (p.154).

Freire and Macedo's argument demonstrates how the white dominant class is determined to use English as the lingua franca to maintain the status quo. Their argument also illustrates the hidden ideological battle over which language is superior or inferior. Of course, through such a battle, the ideological construction of a "superior language" consequently leads to the marginalization of other languages, as it has been the case since colonization. In the remainder of this chapter, I aim to analyze how language is used as a political and ideological construct to misrepresent certain groups in society. To do so, I will draw upon Phillipson's term "linguicism."

Used in the political context of the United States, linguicism might help one better understand why the dominant class uses texts, the language one speaks, the ethnic group and social class to which one belongs, and the country from which one comes to perpetuate their linguistic terror and justify their racist actions against the "other," as evidenced in the following poem:

Ode to the new California

1 I come for visit, get treated regal,
2 So I stay, who care illegal.
3 Cross the border poor and broke,
4 Take the bus, see customs bloke.
5 Welfare say come down no more,
6 We send cash right to your door.
7 Welfare checks they make you wealthy,
8 Medi-Cal it keep you healthy.
9 By and by, I got plenty money,
10 Thank, American working dummy.
11 Write to friends in mother land,
12 Tell them come as fast as can.
13 They come in rags and Chebby trucks,
14 I buy big house with welfare bucks.
15 Fourteen families all move in,
16 Neighbor's patience growing tin.
17 Finally, white guy moves away,
18 I buy his house and then I say,
19 Send your family, they just trash,
20 But they draw more welfare cash.
21 Everything is much good,
22 Soon we own the neighborhood.
23 We have hobby, it is called "breeding,"
24 Welfare pay for baby feeding.
25 Kids need dentist? Wife need pills?
26 We get free, we got no bills.
27 We think America damn good place,
28 Too damn good for white man's race.
28 If they no like us, they can go,
29 Got lots of room in Mexico.

First, it is worth noting that this poem was characterized by the State Assemblyman in California, William J. Knight, as "clever" and "funny" when the legislators' Latino/Latina caucus complained that the poem was racist (Macedo & Bartolome, cited in Zou and Trouba, 1998, p.364). Knight's characterization of the poem is a solid evidence of how words can be manipulated by the dominant group to dehumanize the have-nots. Is it not inhuman and linguistically dishonest to call a poem "clever," and "funny" when it stigmatizes, objectifies, and thereby dehumanizes Mexican immigrants?

As made evident through its multiple verses, this poem is designed to portray Mexican immigrants as alien invaders, pirates, uneducated, and linguistically deficient. Do all Mexican immigrants speak like this: "We think America damn good place/Too damn good for white man's race/ If they no like us, they can go can/Got lots of room in Mexico (lines 27-29)"? Do all Mexican immigrants come to the US "In rags and Chebby trucks and buy house with welfare checks (lines 13-14)"?

Statistically, there has not been any convincing evidence that proves that Mexican immigrants heavily rely on welfare checks or, as stated in the poem, "they draw more welfare cash...." to be functional citizens in the U.S. Unlike the way Mexican immigrants are portrayed as poor immigrants who "buy big house with welfare bucks" (line 14), they have earned a great reputation as being hard workers. Their cheap but reliable labor has been used to keep the motor of the U.S. capitalist machine running. However, ironically, the ideological content of this poem demonizes these immigrants, who have strengthened the U.S. economy with their labor force. The dominant class can target and label Mexican immigrants as "lazy and parasitical welfare recipients (lines, 7, 20, 24)" but they cannot honor them for tremendously contributing to the US economy and losing their lives fighting in wars for oils and political and economic power in which this country has engaged them.

What the linguistic and political cynicism of this poem clearly reveals is how the dominant discourse class has used and manipulated language through written texts as an ideological weapon, to portray a negative image of, and attack the subjectivity of the "other." In short, what the content of this poem teaches us is that language can be used as an ideological tool to normalize various forms of oppressions. Equally dangerous, language has been a strategic tool used by colonial and neocolonial powers to dominate and control not only the linguistic, cultural, economic, and political worlds of subordinate groups but also their minds.

As demonstrated through this chapter, language, ideology, and power are inextricably intertwined. Thus, the battle over which language should be valued and spoken in school and in other settings has nothing to do with the grammatical and syntactical rules of the language but rather with the power that is invested in and the ideology that is embedded in it. That said, those in a powerful position are less likely to stop trying to impose their language on others while manipulating the very same language through texts to misrepresent and dominate certain groups of people in society. The imposition on and use of dominant languages such as English and French to ideologically control and marginalize the "other" is not innocent nor is it a recent phenomenon. As I made clear in this chapter, this politics of linguistic domination goes as far back to the time of colonialism and has been revived through neocolonialism. Thus, the questions become: (1) How can one counter this linguistic domination? (2) How can the "subaltern" (Spivak, 1988) protect their identity that has been attacked? (3) How can they re-appropriate and maintain their language that has been under siege? Finally, how can they regain their voices that have been silenced by white colonizing and neocolonizing class? In my humble view, this can be done if, through dialogue and collective effort, both educators and students deconstruct old western values embedded in canonical texts that have been imposed on them in school. Canonical texts that often do not reflect the subjectivity, the cultural, and linguistic realities of many students and teachers.

CHAPTER 7

RESTERN INTELLECTUALS

The redefinition of their roles in a neocolonial and post-enlightenment era

Are intellectuals an autonomous and independent social group, or does every social group have its own particular specialized category of intellectuals? The problem is a complex one, because of the forms to date by the real historical process of formation of the different categories of intellectuals.

Gramsci, Selections from the prison Notebooks.

The job of the honest intellectual is to help out people who need help; to be part of the people who are struggling for rights and justice. That's what you should be doing. But of course, you don't expect to be rewarded for that.

Chomsky interviewed by Leistyna, Presence of Mind

RESTERN AND WESTERN INTELLECTUALS AND THE ENLIGHTENMENT MOVEMENT

It is unquestionable that intellectuals play an important role in society. Through their scholarly work, they influence how people think and act. While some through their progressive and radical ideas challenge the status quo, others through their conservative thoughts and ideas contribute to maintain it. My goal in this chapter is to analyze what role restern intellectuals and allies play or should play in the fight against the neocolonization of the restern world. Given that the West has the monopoly of the "other world" through conquest, exploitation, colonization, and slavery, Western intellectuals and scientists consequently have been well equipped scientifically to produce quality work. Western intellectuals such as David Hume, John Locke, Adam Smith, Marquis de Condorcet, Baron de Montesquieu, Rousseau, and Voltaire are prime examples. For instance, United States, France, and Haiti's legal system has been greatly influenced by ideas that Baron De Montesquieu (1975) and Jean Jacques Rousseau (1968) articulated in their respective books, *The Spirit of the Laws and The Social Contract*. Moreover, Western intellectuals, such as Voltaire, Hume, and Condorcet have profoundly impacted the world, especially during and after the Enlightenment movement that took place in Europe, particularly in France. As Steven Seidman (1994) observes, "If the Enlighteners were not creators of the scientific revolution, they were its great popularizers and propagandists. Through their writing and speeches, they proved indispensable in spreading the word of science to educated Europeans" (p.21). Through their scientific vision of the world articulated in their scholarly work these intellectuals challenged the Greco-Roman Christian tradition, which has strongly influenced and shaped major institutions in society, such as school, family, and even the state. To paraphrase Walter Rodney (1972) during the colonization era, Greco-Roman Christian was wrongly used by the European colonialist power to enslave and dominate the "other." Using the catholic religion as the symbol of salvation and purification, Christopher Columbus, the messenger of Queen Elizabeth of Spain, duped, exploited, and murdered millions of Indigenous people in Central, South America, and in the Caribbean. While his murderous legacy continues to cause economic, political, and psychological damage to the descendents of people he wiped out, ironically Christopher Columbus has been seen and glorified as the brave discoverer of the so-called new world, which he exploited and destroyed.

Moreover, within the Greco-Roman Christian Church in France, the clergy used religion to lie to people, monopolize power and wealth, and maintain social and economic inequalities. As the powerful ambassador of the church, the clergy was able to influence the political power structure and the state apparatus of European countries, such as France. The clergy was not alone in using religion for its own imperial interest. Colonial European countries such as France, Great Britain, and Portugal used religion as a weapon to justify and maintain colonization in Africa, as Rodney (1972) made clear in his classic book, *How Europe Underdeveloped Africa*. Worst of all, religion has been used by the Roman Catholic Church as an ideological weapon to brainwash people's minds, including students, so that they would accept the status quo. In my view, the Catholic Church was and still is in a powerful position to do so because it is believed to be the source and the depository of canonical truth.

However, with the advent of the enlightenment movement, an old world was about to end, and the path for a new world was on its way to be paved. The church was no longer seen as the legitimate and reliable source of truth. Its power was challenged, weakened, and even destroyed by the fresh, new, and revolutionary ideas that stemmed from and were propagated by the philosophers and scientists of the enlightenment movement. It was no longer a question of believing blindly in the clergy, for people came to the realization that science, rather than merely religious faith, should guide their actions. Asymmetrical power relations that the Church supported and maintained between the powerful and the powerless were questioned and threatened by revolutionary ideas and actions of Voltaire, Montesqueu, and Condorcet. Thus, the Enlighteners with their novel ideas opened a new horizon and shed some light on the world that was shadowed by the concentrated power of the Roman Catholic Church.

It is undeniable that authoritative figures of the enlightenment movement fought against the injustice and aristocracy, which were reigned within the Catholic Church. It is unquestionable that they also stood up for a better world informed and led by reason and genial ideas of liberty, equality, and fraternity. While, on the one hand, Montesquieu and Rousseau greatly contributed to and impacted the legal system worldwide, Voltaire and Condorcet, on the other hand, produced an impressive body of social ideas which opened and continues opening people's eyes on the social injustice perpetuated by the dominant class in society. I personally have been strongly influenced by ideas that Rousseau, Montesquieu, and Voltaire articulated through their scholarly work. In fact, their ideas have helped me have a better understanding of the world.

Through the lens of their theoretical framework, I have come to understand the world as a place where the powerful control the wealth at the expense of the powerless; a place where almost everything is falling apart due to educational, economic, social, and political inequalities; a place where a privileged powerful minority often robs possibilities from certain groups of people based on their gender, race/ethnicity, social class, national origin, and linguistic backgrounds; and finally a place where the powerful and the oppressors have plenty of voice, which is highly valued and heard, whereas the voice of the powerless and the oppressed has been silenced. By making such an argument, I do not mean that the world is not at the same time full of possibilities and hope. My contention is that this hope has been unfortunately rendered hopeless by imperialism, neocolonialism, racism, sexism, classism, and ableism.

Philosophers and critical theorists, such as Jean Paul Sartre and John Locke, were influenced and inspired by thinkers like Voltaire, David Hume, and Montesquieu; so were prominent intellectuals and sociologists, such as Karl Marx, August Comte, and Emile Durkheim. Precisely, novel ideas that the enlighteners articulated through their scholarly work challenged, years later, members of the Frankfurt School, such as Jurgen Habermas, Herbert Marcus, Theodor Adorno, and Max Horheimer, to see the world not through the eyes of religion but through science. Furthermore, through their scholarly work, the Enlighteners and succeeding Western intellectuals, such as Voltaire, David Hume, Rousseau, Montesquieu, and Thomas Jefferson, eloquently made an appeal for liberty and freedom and advocated for a world that is built upon the establishment of a legal system and a social contract that cherish and protect people's freedom, rights, and liberty. It goes without saying that the ideas of the enlighteners have undoubtedly a universally human character attached to them. Consequently, one might be convinced that these intellectuals advocated for the benefits of all human beings on earth. However, what I find problematic, contradictory, and hypocritical about the enlighteners and their successors is that, the same Voltaire, Thomas Jefferson, and David Hume, who fought for a scientific understanding of the world and made convincing appeals for sacred inalienable human rights such as liberty, equality, justice, and happiness, also fervently supported the enslavement of black people, whom they declared to be inferior and unintelligent. As Galeano (2000) observed:

> Voltaire, anticlerical writer, advocate of tolerance and reason claims that Blacks are inferior to Europeans but superiors to apes. Carolus Linnaeus, Classifier of plants and animals maintains that the Black is a vagabond, lazy, negligent, indolent, and dissolute morals. And David Hume, Master of human understanding declares that the Black might develop certain attributes of human beings, the way parrot manages to speak a few words. (p. 62).

79

Such a racist argument articulated by Voltaire, Linnaeus, and Hume directly excludes blacks from the social and political project for which the enlighteners
fought. It also clearly denies black people the human rights that these thinkers
wrote about and fought for in their battle against the Catholic Church. Simply put,
the black, the colonized were not included in the agenda of these European intellectuals as they were rebelling against the ignorance perpetuated by the aristocracy
within the Catholic Church and the clergy in Europe. Their battle for a so-called
better world free from oppression and ignorance was launched for the exclusive
benefit of white Europeans, particularly the white colonialists. While Montesquieu
and Voltaire were writing about the need to have a world freed from oppression,
subjugation, and control of the Roman Catholic Church, millions of African descendents were being enslaved in Haiti. Yet, nowhere in their work did these authors suggest to take a stand against the inhuman condition of the slaves in Haiti.
Nor did they write about or stand up for Indigenous people's rights in
South/Central/North America and the Caribbean who were murdered by the Spaniards.

Years later during the French revolution, house slaves in Haiti most certainly
overheard French colonizers talking about justice and freedom. However, these
words were empty and meaningless to the imported African slaves in Haiti who
were oppressed by the same country, France, where the battle for freedom, justice,
equality, and a better world was taking place. Of course, one cannot and should not
dismiss the work and effort of intellectuals of the enlightenment movement who
fought for a world that should be scientifically oriented, free from ignorance, su-
perstition, and the concentrated power of the Catholic Church. However, given the
social class background and status of these French intellectuals, I wonder if the
underlying reasons to fight against the Catholic Church were not to overthrow this
institution so that they could have access to the same type of power the clergy had.
In fact, this was the outcome of the French revolution, which was influenced by the
ideas of the enlightenment. That is, the bourgeois class that revolted against the
noble and clerical class turned out to be equally oppressive of the lower classes
once they took power. To some degree they reproduced the asymmetrical power
relation that the clergy maintained for decades. This confirms the idea that social
movements led by bureaucrat intellectuals is usually limited in that it fails to serve
the interest of marginalized groups in society. In the case of the enlightenment
movement it is doubtful that it was intended to serve the interest of all humankind
given non-Europeans, particularly people of color were not part of the agenda of
the enlighteners. The enlightenment movement clearly was a movement whose
objective was solely to serve the interest of the bourgeois European class. This is,
in my view, the danger that lies in social movements led by the bourgeois class,
which historically has not proven to be a revolutionary class, due to its selfish interest in maintaining the status quo. In this sense, Marx and Engels (1945) are right
when they argued that only the proletarian class can truly be a revolutionary class,
for this is a class that has nothing to lose but all to gain. In his book, *State and
Revolution*, Lenin (1943) illustrated Marx and Engels' idea about the two opposing
classes. Lenin stated:

The exploiting classes need political rule in order to maintain exploitation, i.e., in the selfish interests of an insignificant minority, and against the vast majority of the people. The exploited classes need political rule in order completely to abolish all exploitation, i.e., in the interests of the vast majority of the people, and against the insignificant minority consisting of the slave-owners of modern times-the landlords and the capitalists. (p. 22).

Although the intellectual bourgeois class, who were the leading figures of the enlightenment movement, might not have been the exploiting class per say, they needed, as Lenin made clear, "political rule" in order to maintain the status quo. Thus, to echo Lenin (1943) "what is to be done?" to unveil the hypocritical nature of the enlightenment movement and its negative impact on the restern world? Should restern intellectuals and western allied intellectuals work together to challenge the scholarly works of influential European enlighteners that have been used in both the "modern" and "postmodern" world? How would western and restern intellectuals support each other, and work on an equal footing in this project? What has been or should be the role of intellectuals both living in restern and the western world in countering the cultural hegemonic, economic and political domination of the West on the Rest. It is to an analysis of the role that restern intellectuals and allied intellectuals have played and need to continuously play to change the socio-political and economic paradigm of such an "uneven world" (Radhakrishnan, 2003) that I am turning next.

WHAT SHOULD BE THE ROLE OF INTELLECTUALS, PARTICULARLY RESTERN INTELLECTUALS, IN A NEOCOLONIAL ERA?

First, it is worth making the distinction between territorial conservative intellectuals and borderless intellectuals. I argue that while, on the one hand, territorial conservative intellectuals are often the servants of the dominant class, borderless intellectuals, on the other, write about and speak against social, economic, and political inequalities perpetuated by this class. Their actions and political stances are radical and humanist by nature and thereby transcend the borders of their socio-economic and political milieu. Critical thinkers, such as Antonio Gramsci, Edward Said, Antenor Firmin, Howard Zinn, Walter Rodney, Paulo Freire, Sonia Nieto, Henry Giroux, Frantz Fanon, Amical Cabrar, Aime Cesaire, Arundhati Roy, Noam Chomsky, and Eqbal Ahmad, to name only a few, are borderless intellectuals par excellence. Their intellectual activism has transcended the border of their native lands and impacted the entire international intellectual community. The legacy they left behind and/or they will be leaving behind will teach humankind the following lesson: It takes love, courage, sacrifice, dedication, persistence, and consistency to be a borderless intellectual. In this context, it is worth alluding here to Said's praise of a borderless intellectual's scholarly and activist work and legacy, Eqbal Ahmad. The late Said, recognizing the undying contribution of Eqbal Ahmad to the world, cherishes his intellectual courage in the following terms:

One of the remarkable things about him (i.e., Ahmad) was that even though he crossed more borders and traversed more boundaries than most people, Eqbal was reassuringly himself in each new place, new situation, new context. This was not at all a matter of ethnic or religious identity, nor did it have much to do with the habitual stability we associate with solid citizens. Rather, Eqbal's special blend of intellectual brilliance and courage, supernally accurate analysis, and consistently humane and warm presence made of him, to paraphrase from Rudyard Kipling's Kim, a friend of the whole world. (Cited from the foreword by Edward W. Said, In Confronting Empire, Eqbal Ahmad, 2000).

As Said's comments illustrate, borderless intellectuals like Ahmad are an inspiration for future borderless intellectuals. In fact, I would argue that borderless intellectuals are a beacon for those who dare to transcend ethnic, linguistic, racial, and social boundaries surrounding their socio-economic and political milieu in order to fight for a universal human cause. Borderless intellectuals have of course been strategic in their political acts in the sense that they know when to stand up to speak against social inequalities. They also have been proven to be courageous and determined when faced with multiple challenges and adversity in life. For example, Antonio Gramsci (1971) never stopped writing about and fighting for what he believed in while he was incarcerated. He took risks that not only caused him to be incarcerated but also cost his political career, affected his family, and ultimately cost him his life. Although grave, I believe these risks are worth taking because intellectuals should not wait to be told why, when, and where to intervene while evil forces of neocolonialism, neoliberalism, racism, sexism, classism, and ableism are affecting humanity. In my opinion, this is what differentiates borderless intellectuals from other intellectuals and makes them unforgettable and immortal in the historical archive of the world.

Like Frantz Fanon, Paulo Freire, Antenor Firmin, Walter Rodney, and Amilcar Cabral, other intellectuals in and from the restern countries need to act as borderless activist intellectuals. My contention is that restern intellectuals should not be the receptacles, transmitters, and executers of ideas articulated by conservative western intellectuals. Rather, they should try to act as authentic intellectuals who challenge these ideas. Equally important, they should involve in global political and social movements aimed to combat misrepresentation of and servile cultural alienation of postcolonial subjects living both in the restern world and in the Diaspora. Finally, as Thomas Sankara (1984) contends:

They must understand that the battle for an ideology that serves the needs of the disinherited masses is not vain. But they must understand, too, that they can only become credible on an international level by being genuinely creative-by portraying a faithful image of their people, an image conducive to carrying out fundamental change in political and social conditions and to wrenching our countries from foreign domination and exploitation, which leave us no other perspective than bankruptcy. (p. 88).

As Sankara suggested, internationally restern intellectuals should act as ambassadors of their countries who are willing to engage in an ideological, political, and intellectual battle to represent and defend their countries. Nationally, they should play the role of intellectual vanguards who are tenaciously fighting against foreign cultural invasion. Both nationally and internationally, restern intellectuals should work tirelessly to heighten and defend the national dignity and culture of their countries.

Historically, one of the biggest challenges that countries with a historical burden of colonization have been facing is to salvage their culture, which was and still is to a certain extent perceived as an alienating or a savage culture. It is, therefore, imperative that both restern intellectuals and ordinary people who lived under colonization and/or have had to deal with the aftermath of it redefine who they are, for the cultural image that is attributed to them by the colonizers and neocolonizers is an image of savagery and of the uncivilized. This is well captured by Arundhati Roy (2001) when she maintains that: "Fifty years after independence, India is still struggling with the legacy of colonialism, still flinching from the 'cultural insult'. As citizens we're still caught up in the business of 'disproving' the white world's definition of us" (p.13).

As Roy's statement suggests, even though formerly restern colonized countries such as Haiti and India have gained their independence, they continue facing the challenge to make the West respect their culture that is often looked down upon. Cultural autonomy and identities of many formerly colonized countries have been in jeopardy due perhaps to a lack of unshakable cultural resistance of intellectuals living in these countries against the cultural imperialism of the West. With that said, I suggest that restern intellectuals play the role of cultural vanguards in their intellectual fight against western cultural invasion of their countries. But can they take on that role if their intellectual work has merely been reduced to teaching, writing, publishing, and lecturing at conferences?

The cultural vanguard role of restern intellectuals, as I conceive it, should not be limited to teaching, writing, publishing, and lecturing at conferences. It should also consist of reaching out to the poor and helping them to be better prepared ideologically for potential radical social changes. Restern intellectuals can start playing that cultural vanguard role by helping the masses organize cultural events where, together with them, they explore and discuss the important interconnection between nation, state, and culture. Moreover, through the sharing and exchange of ideas, cultural vanguard restern intellectuals can guide and help the masses to use cultural artifacts, such as songs rooted in their culture and history, as a form of cultural and historical resistance to fight against western neocolonial cultural, economic, and political dominations. Equally important, on a national level, cultural vanguard restern intellectuals ought to make the effort to fight against obsolete cultural practices and social norms that contribute to the marginalization and oppression of certain group of people in society, such as gay men, lesbians, bisexual people, transgendered people, and people with disabilities in the restern world. My contention is that the fight against any oppression such as neocolonialism should also entail fighting against all other forms of oppressions, starting with the ones that occur at one's home or native land.

I am fully aware that what I am articulating here might be a real challenge for restern intellectuals, including myself, who have been educated in the West and immersed in western discourses. For this category of intellectuals, they would have to "reinvent themselves," as Freire (1970) suggested, in order to play the cultural vanguard role. Or else, they may end up regurgitating what they have been taught in Western universities in terms of western discourses and ideology. Another huge challenge that awaits western educated restern intellectuals is to find ways in which to make their language accessible to both students and the uneducated masses in the restern world.

By language, I do not mean simply words uttered, nor do I refer to syntactical and morphological aspects of it. Rather, I am referring to the ideological aspect of it, the values, beliefs, ideology, and norms that are embedded in languages like English and French, in which restern intellectuals have been educated. Eqbal Ahmad (2000) understood the ideological component and implications of language. In the case of the Algerian school system, Ahmad maintained:

> Higher education is supposed to have arabized. The reality was, the Algerian independent state remained organically tied to France and to the international market. Therefore the local language, Arabic, was devalued. So you have a situation in which you have higher education without a language. You can't impart higher education without a consistent language policy. That contributed to a decline in education. Second, we all inherited a colonial system of higher education. These post-colonial governments had no will or desire to introduce an alternative system of education. The rhetoric and the structure they announced was that of independence. The reality was that of higher education based on colonial premises and systems. The educational system in this new setting of post-colonial statehood became increasingly dysfunctional because it came under opposing, contradictory pressures. (pp. 19-20).

Expanding upon Ahmad's argument, I shall contend that in order not to culturally alienate students by assimilating them into western culture, it is imperative that western-educated restern intellectuals dewesternize their language and knowledge so that they can be accessible to students and the uneducated masses in restern countries. Furthermore, if restern intellectuals both in the native land and abroad are serious about contributing to the cultural, educational, and political advancement of their countries, they ought to take a stance against governments which, influenced by western capitalist countries, invest a lot more in the national army than in school material and equipment, such as computers, laboratories, and books.

All in all, restern intellectuals have a double task to assume. On an international scale, they need to talk back to western power that refuses to treat them on an equal footing, despite their intellectual, academic, and professional achievements. While it is crucial that they continue striving for intellectual excellence, they should not lose sight of the importance of fighting against western imperialism, in order to ensure that the national and cultural dignity and political autonomy of restern countries can be respected. Such a noble but immense task might sound idealistic to restern intellectuals who have allowed their voices to be silenced by the western power structure in order to secure a tenured position at a university. Those who chose to sell their intelligence, knowledge, and human dignity to huge western capitalist corporations also might ridicule this. Raising consciousness among this group of intellectuals will be a huge challenge, for they may have no interest in changing the status quo from which they have been profiting. In fact, these intellectuals often behave as the restern version of western colonialists, whose goal is to profit from the neocolonial system apparatus. These intellectuals, as Sartre (1965) pointed out, "will change nothing and will serve no one, but will succeed only in finding moral comfort in malaise." However, one should not lose hope, for as Freire (1993) reminds us, "it is imperative that we maintain hope even when the harshness of reality may suggest the opposite." We should indeed maintain hope because there are still very few borderless intellectuals who, despite being marginalized by the bureaucracy of such institutions as schools, continue to engage in a tenuous fight for a balance in the power relations between the western and the restern world. Unfortunately, these very few intellectuals have not gotten enough recognition for their courageous political and intellectual actions.

On a national scale, restern intellectuals should work tirelessly to influence and, if necessary, infiltrate the political body of the country they live in, for sometimes the surest and best way to challenge the political power structure of any country is by penetrating it. Penetrating or, rather, influencing the political make up of the country by restern intellectuals will serve, in my view, four important purposes. First, they will be in a better position to challenge drastic economic and political decisions that governments in restern countries make on behalf of the poor. Such decisions, if not challenged by intellectuals who possess or have a clear sense of "historical conscience" (Diop, 1991), might have ruinous consequences on the masses in the restern world. Cheick Anta Diop, the prominent Senegalese intellectual, eloquently explicates the significance of and vital role historical conscience plays in the cultural protection of a people, as well as in the historical renaissance of a nation. Diop (1991) maintains:

> The historical conscience, through the feeling of cohesion that it creates, constitutes the safest and the most solid shield of cultural security for a people. This is why every people seeks only to know and to live their true history well, to transmit its memory to their descendents. The essential thing, for people, is to rediscover the thread that connects them to their most remote ancestral past. In the face of cultural aggression of all sorts, in the face of all disintegrating factors of the outside world, the most efficient cultural weapon with which a people can arm itself is this feeling of historical continuity. The erasing, the destruction of the historical conscience also has been since time began part of the techniques of colonization, enslavement, and debasement of peoples. (p. 212).

Secondly, as Diop suggested, by using a historical conscience as part of the political framework of their intellectual activism, restern intellectuals will be well equipped ideologically to counter the hegemonic, imperialist, political, and cultural attack of western empires against their countries. Third, restern intellectuals who manage to infiltrate the government apparatus will be in the best position to play an active role in any democratic and political process that leads to the liberation of the poor from the prison of poverty and inequality. Finally, by being at the center of the political debate of their country, restern intellectuals can play a major role in fighting against any occupation of their native land by western imperial powers. As Fanon (1963) observes:

> The native intellectual nevertheless sooner or later will realize that you do not show proof of your nation from its culture but that you substantiate its existence the fight which the people wage against the forces of occupation (p. 223).

I shall argue that if restern intellectuals are to earn a national reputation as cultural vanguards of their countries, they first need to culturally be immersed in their own culture and work hard to salvage it from western cultural invasion. And to earn an international reputation as borderless intellectuals, they should not be afraid to take risks to tell dangerous truths about social, racial, economic, and political inequalities of Western neocolonizing powers. Nor should they be afraid of engaging in the defense of human rights wherever they happen to be violated. Until they have cultivated moral clarity and courage to do so, they will simply be "servants of power" (Chomsky, 2005) who, throughout history, have been serving the corporate interest of western imperial powers and that of a small national dominant group who have monopolized the wealth of the restern world.

CHAPTER 8

RESTERN WOMEN UNDER WESTERN GAZE

A critical sociohistorical analysis of their struggles from the colonial to the neoliberal era

While feminists have been involved in the antiglobalization movement from the start, however, this has not been a major organizing locus for women's movements nationally in the West/North. It has, however, always been a locus of struggle for women of the Third World/South because of their location. Again, this contextual specificity should constitute the larger vision. Women of the Two-Thirds World have always organized against the devastations of globalized capital, just as they have always historically organized anticolonial and antiracist movements. In this sense they have always spoken for humanity as a whole.

Chandra Mohanty

What "feminism" means to women of color is different from what it means to white women. Because of our collective histories, we identify more closely with international Third World sisters than with white feminist women...A global feminism, one that reaches beyond patriarchal political divisions and national ethnic boundaries, can be formulated from a new political perspective.

Alice Chai

In the first two chapters, I briefly talked about the socio-economic and political situations of women, particularly poor restern women in Haiti and in India. While I don't claim to fully understand the historical journey of and the economic, social, political, and religious situations of these women, in this chapter I aim to elaborate on this journey and analyze these situations. I shall briefly analyze how restern women were treated during colonization and slavery. In addition, I shall analytically link restern women's socio-economic and political situations to the effect of globalization, which is, in my view, the running capitalist machine of western neocolonial and neoliberal agenda. By so doing, I aim to challenge assumptions that have been made about restern women's complex realities. Finally, I shall demonstrate how, the legacy of colonialism alongside Western neoliberal economic and political policies have impacted these women. The central argument of this paper is that, as transnational Western capitalist corporations are leaving Western territories to go overseas in search of cheaper labor, the exploitation and abuse of human rights of restern factory workers become an undeniable reality. Hence, my focus here will primarily be on the condition of poor working class women although the plight of women belonging to higher social status will also be incorporated in my analysis. Given my familiarity with the historical and political context of women's struggle in the Caribbean, in Africa, particularly in Haiti and Algeria, I will mainly situate my analysis of the economic, social and political situations of restern women in the Caribbean and African context. Simply stated, examples of Caribbean and African women, especially factory workers and farmers will be used as cases in point to substantiate my arguments. But first off I wish to position myself by delineating my background and explaining various factors that led me to become interested in issues related to women's struggles.

SEL POSITIONING

I am a heterosexual black man who was born and grew up in the Caribbean where women, particularly lesbians, have been doubly oppressed due to homophobia and sexism. As a young boy, I remember having in my house seasonal female maids who were paid to help my sisters cook, clean, and wash my cloths and those of my father and brother. Regrettably, at no time, did I ever question why these maids were always women, but not men or both. Although I never mistreated them, I never felt that I could identify myself with these maids. I was simply socialized to believe that they were not like me. In other words, I was taught to simply look at them as maids who were uneducated and were from lower social class. I was never taught nor was I ever encouraged by my teachers, parents or friends to interrogate why they were uneducated and belonged to lower social class. I merely accepted the status quo.

In 2005, twelve years after I left my native land to migrate to the US, I decided to join an advanced certificate program in the women studies department at the University of Massachusetts at Amherst, where I am currently pursuing a doctorate degree in education. I decided to do so because I felt that it was time to stop speculating about women's economic and sociopolitical conditions. I concluded if I wanted to support the feminist movement I first have to educate myself about women's struggles. Prior to joining the certificate program, where I had the privilege to be exposed to and familiar with feminist theories and discourses, I used to reproduce sexist behavior which I learned through social interactions with both men and women in my social milieu.

In Haiti, approximately 60 percent of the workforce comprises of women, who are "Madan Sara" (street venders or women merchants), farmers, and factory workers. While working long hours as Madan Sara in the street or as farmers in their farms or as factory workers in factories, they were still expected to take care of the house (clean, cook, iron their husband cloths) and their children. Protesting against this kind of oppression was seen and taken as a sign of bad motherhood and parenting. Those who dared to resist, including some of my mother's cousins, were often beaten and ridiculed. Although Haitian women constitute the majority of the Haitian population and, more importantly, the backbone of the country and their family, they have been the most marginalized groups in the Haitian society. They are perceived and treated as weak, powerless, and as a minority although numerically they outnumbered Haitian men, a weak, poorly treated minority who is nevertheless the pillar of Haitian economy.

Having witnessed the physical, emotional, and economic sabotage of restern women in my social milieu, I have since been wanting to explore the inhuman living and working conditions of these women. One of the questions that has preoccupied my mind for more than a decade is the following: Has the situation of restern women gotten better, worse, or remained the same since colonization? My contention is that to better understand the current working condition of women living in the restern requires, one needs to have a sound historical understanding of the living and working conditions of women during slavery and colonization.

RESTERN WOMEN DURING SLAVERY AND COLONIZATION

During the French colonization in Haiti, female slaves endured the most brutal exploitation and subjugation in the colony. Like their husbands, they had to work in the plantation from dawn to sunset. However, unlike them, they were often brutally raped by their colonizers. In addition, many of them had miscarriage, as a result of poor diet and heavy labor. After long days of labor in the plantation, they still had to clean, and take care of their enslaved children—except those whose children were taken away from them and sent to other plantations. Despite their major sacrifice and hard work during and after colonization and slavery, women were dismissed and relegated to a subordinate position in society.

During colonization, no colonized subject was exempt from the atrocity of the colonial system, for it was a system that dehumanized everyone, including, to a certain extent, poor colonialists who were called "petit blanc" as Memmi (1965) and Fanon (1963, 1965) articulated in their scholarly work. However, women were worse off than men in the way they were treated during colonization. Here, to paraphrase Stoler (2002), I am referring to colonized women, but certainly not white female Europeans who, despite their subordinating status in comparison to that of their spouse, occupied a privileged position in the colony. As Stoler (2002) notes: "…European women in these colonies experienced the cleavages of racial dominance and internal social distinctions very differently than men precisely because of their ambiguous positions, as both subordinates in colonial hierarchies and as agents of empire in their own right"(p.41). In fact, in the words of Federici (2004), "Regardless of their social origin, white women were upgraded, or married off within the ranks of the white power structure, and whenever possible they became owners of slaves themselves, usually female ones, employed for domestic work" (p.108). To take Federici's argument a step further, I would argue that even poor white European women, who were forced out of poverty to migrate to the Caribbean, were better off economically, socially, and politically than indigenous women who were treated as the "other" in their own land. For example, while colonized indigenous women were doing housework, they had to work outside their home in the plantation to enrich the colonizer.

Before colonization, women lived in societies that were community oriented. As Engels (1884) made clear in *The Origin of the Family and Private Propriety, and the State* women played a significant role in their communal society. They greatly contributed to the economy of their communal society; they were trusted and independent and took part in the decision making process in their respective communal society. Along those lines, (Federici, 2004) maintains, "Pre-conquest American women had their organizations, their socially recognized spheres of activity and, while not equal to men, they were considered complementary to them in their contribution to the family and society." However, with the advent of colonization, which is the economic driven tool of capitalism, women's social and economic positions drastically changed. They were no longer treated as independent and important members of their society. They were oppressed by all accounts. This is well captured by Kerr (2006), who notes:

> The 'inferiorization' of indigenous peoples connotes a double jeopardy for women: not only were they relegated to a subordinate position as the 'other' by the colonizers, but they also suffered the loss of social position with their own communities with the advent of European colonization. (p. 295).

Moreover, while under the subjugation of the Spaniards, the French, and the British, enslaved and colonized indigenous women were forced to abort their babies and/or commit suicide as a form of resistance to the colonial power. Federici (2004), paraphrasing Silverblatt (1987) and Hemming (1970), points out, "In the Andes, some committed suicide and killed their male children, presumably to prevent them from ongoing to the mines and also out of disgust, apparently, for the mistreatment inflicted upon them by their male relatives." In addition, indigenous women were constantly concerned about being raped as it has been the case in countries such as Soudan, particularly in Darfur, Haiti, Afghanistan, and Liberia, where thousands of women have been raped. They had to hide when they heard the colonialist was coming their way. All of this human atrocity took place upon the arrival and the settlement of European countries, such as France, Spain, and Great Britain in South and Central America, in the Caribbean, and in Africa.

The European colonization of these continents has crippled the social, economic, and political situations of Caribbean, Asian, Latina, and African women. While the human dignity of these women was decreased, their heavy labor was increased. Furthermore, while at home they had to deal with abuse coming from their angry and exploited husbands, who often took their frustration and anger out on them. In the plantation they had to cope with the sexual assault of their colonialist and even of the male Indians. Federeci (2004) notes, "In the European fantasy, America itself was a reclining naked woman seductively inviting the approaching white stranger. At times, it was the 'Indian' men themselves who delivered their female kin to the priests or encomenderos in exchange for some economic reward or a public post."

With regard to domestic violence, the body and spirit of enslaved indigenous and black women was the channel through which their husband released their frustration and anger caused by a colonial system that treated them like sub-humans, like beasts. Not yet ready to confront and attack the colonizer who subjugated them, when returning home from a long day of heavy labor, the colonized men took out their frustrations and anger out on their wives, who were perceived and treated as weak and thus, indefensible. Fanon (1963) argued that under colonization, colonized men often brutally fought with their colonized brothers and sisters to release their accumulative frustration and anger the colonial system caused them. And yet, women who were abused by their husbands were often the ones who had to lie to protect the latter when the colonialists wanted to capture and hang them.

As demonstrated in the film, *The Battle of Alger,* during the Algerian liberation movement, colonized Algerian women often had to lie to save the life of Algerian men, particularly their husbands, who were fighting the French colonizers. They used their veil to fool the French soldiers so that they could deliver important messages to male Algerian militants. Their veil, which held and still holds religious and cultural meanings, was transformed into a tool of resistance against the French colonial power. In *A Dying Colonialism*, Fanon (1965) explained the vital role that the veil worn by Algerian women played in the Algerian liberation movement. Fanon stated:

> We shall see that this veil, one of the elements of the traditional Algerian garb, was to become the bone of contention in a grandiose battle, on account of which the occupation forces were to mobilize their most powerful and most varied resources, and in the course of which the colonized were to display a surprising force of inertia. Taken as a whole, colonial society, with its values, its areas of strength, and its philosophy, reacts to the veil in a rather homogenous way. (pp. 37 & 38).

In addition to the veil, Algerian women also used their gender and sexuality against the French colonizers, who perceived and treated them as sexual objects, to cross gates and setup bombs in nightclubs and restaurants where the French colonizers frequently went to dance and eat. Given the gendered structure of the Algerian society, the meaning of the veil was not symbolically embedded in its physical construct. Rather, it was attached to the femininity and innocence by which Algerian women were characterized. Simply put, the veil was feminized and gendered. However, while it can be argued that the veil that Muslim women carry can perpetuate sexism and gendered unequal power relations among Muslim men and women, it is undeniable that it played a significant role in the Algerian liberation movement.

Yet, despite their contribution to and the great sacrifice they made to set their country free from French colonization, the social, economic, and political conditions of Algerian women have not been improved. Who has had access to power after the independence of Algeria? Since Algeria became independent, have Algerian women been liberated from the abuse of their husbands, whom they protected during the war of liberation? How many of Algerian women who are integral members of the economic and political affairs of Algeria? To cast light on these questions, I wish to allude here to the reaction of a few Algerian coworkers with whom I engaged in a dialogue about the social, political, and economic situations of Algerian women in a post-colonized Algerian society. I challenged them by asking: how many women in your country hold key political positions? They responded by arguing, "Women should not be involved in politics because their children need their presence and support in the house? They went on to state, "besides, politics make people lie, and Muslim women should not lie. That's against the Koran." Obviously, it will be dangerous to draw a conclusion about the social, economic, and political situations of Algerian women based on the opinion of three individual Algerian men. However, their expectation of what Algerian women should be doing or not doing as "woman" reflects clearly their narrowed sexist view, which some men cross-culturally might share.

For example, my Algerian coworkers' positions are in line with the position of many Haitian men that I have known. These Haitian men, including some of my male cousins and good friends, believe that women should not be involved in politics. They have claimed that women are not strong enough to govern or lead a country. Interestingly enough, the Haitian political apparatus mirrors what my cousins and friends have articulated about women's role and positions in society. Although Haitian women numerically outnumber Haitian men, in the political body of the country they are underrepresented. In fact, I would venture saying that they are invisible. Only a very few privileged Haitian women have managed to occupy some positions at the political level in Haiti after the departure of the Duvalier regime. Because of the way women's roles have been defined in Haiti, women who dare to run for office are often ridiculed and, consequently, do not receive the support that they need to counter men political hegemony. Myrland Marnigat (2006), the first Haitian woman who ever held a senatorial seat in Haiti, brilliantly captured this undeniable reality. She stated, "To raise the money for a campaign or travel to talk to voters is a genuine ordeal for Haitian women. Only exceptional women can ever try to get the credibility necessary to be politically active."

As demonstrated above, women in the restern world to a certain extent continue to experience similar economic, social, and political amputations that colonized and enslaved women experienced during colonization and slavery. While today restern women are not physically and mentally enchained like the slaved, colonized women, they continue experiencing social, political, and economic isolations and dominations perpetuated by men in power. Placing my Algerian and Haitian friends' statement on a global context, it can be argued that it essentially reflects sexist male positions that have been held and worked against women's interests, human dignity and subjectivity. As their position reveals, it is the norm and therefore is expected of Muslim and Haitian men to be involved in politics, but not women. In other words, it is expected of Algerian men to be involved in politics to lie while women are forbidden to do so. This attitude towards Algerian and Haitian women romanticizes the role of women in society, thereby perpetuates gender inequality. Simply put, it falsely portrays women as pure angels while contributing to the maintenance of the patriarchal status quo. In short, my Haitian and Algerian's men statement reflects a male dominated discourse that has been reproduced throughout many Caribbean, African, Latin American, and Asian countries.

In the Caribbean, particularly in Haiti, historically women have been politically marginalized. Even though Haiti became independent in 1804, Haitian women were not allowed to vote until 1957. Despite their contribution to the social and economic advancement of the country, it was not until in 1987, a year after the Haitian dictator Jean Claude Duvalier was forced to leave power, that Haitian women started to have their voice heard. However, men have been the ones governing Haiti until in 1990 when Ertha Pascal-Trouilot, the first female Haitian high court judge, temporarily help power for about a year as a result of political disturbance that paralyzed the whole country. Although shortly lasted, her presidency has inspired and strengthened many Haitian women to be politically active. In fact, since her presidency, women's movement in Haiti became visible to the public sphere. Some organizations, such as the association of Haitian women (AFAB) and ENFOFANM- an Organization for the Defense of Women's Rights led by Haitian women, have been for the last decade or so defending Haitian women's rights both in Haiti and in the Diaspora. Unfortunately, too often these organizations are not adequately funded and are overshadowed by a political structure that is male dominated and remains irresponsive and inept to the human and political rights of women.

While I do not intend here to universalize or homogenize the political situation of Caribbean, African, Latin American, and Asian women, it is safe to argue that women in these continents historically share similar political hardship and isolation. Many women, such as Rigoberta Menchu and Winnie Mandela, have been at the forefront of social and political movements in Latin America and Africa to fight and advocate for both African and Indigenous men and women rights. However, although they have gained some international recognition and fame, they have not been given the opportunity to govern their country. Despite their political dynamism and activism, it has been men in their country who have gained access to political power.

Women have been conveniently used to serve the political interest of Caribbean, African, Latin American, and Asian men. Up until now, no male leaders, not even the self proclaimed progressive ones in these continents, have opened space for women to occupy key governmental positions such as vice presidents or prime ministers. Yet, these leaders continue talking about democracy, equal rights, and the protection of human rights: Democracy, equal rights, and protection of human rights for whom? And who benefits from these rights? Is it not a group of male leaders who have convinced African, Caribbean, Latin American, and Asian women to vote for them during election, so they can get elected or reelected while the status quo remains intact? Whereas these women have been used for men's political gains, respect for their human rights is yet to become a reality. Put in simple terms, women in the Caribbean, Africa, Latin America, and in Asia have been used as political plays by men to stay in power. The gender gap, which puts these and their male counterparts in unequal power relations, has yet to be bridged.

For example, Ewig (1999) recounts that, Nicaraguan women who played a major role in the revolutionary struggle against the Somozists and in the post-revolutionary period have continued to fight for their human rights. However, they have experienced gender inequality at all levels. For instance, during the revolution they played an important role in the military. However, after the revolution, this was no longer the case. Ewig, paraphrasing Whisnant (1995), states that, "Even in the military, where women had played a significant role during the revolution, women's subsequent participation was limited. Within a year of the revolutionary victory, women dropped from a third of the armed forces to less than 10 percent, with only 3 women among the 74 top commanders and 13 in the officer training corps of 231" (Whisnant 1995, 419-21, in Ewig, 1999). Ewig also reports that in the civil society Nicaraguan women have been mostly able to organize themselves through nongovernmental organizations (NGOs), to address issues of concern to women, issues such as Nicaraguan women's rights to abortion, which has been recently banned by the Nicaraguan government under the influence of the Catholic Church. Despite Nicaraguan women's vital contribution to end the dictatorship of the Somozas, their social and economic conditions have not improved like they may have wished. As one former Sandinista feminist activist who was interviewed by Ewig stated, "Sandinismo was revolutionary... in society, in the socialization of property. But in private life, women were property. It wasn't revolutionary in this sense, within the family" (Ewig, 1999).

Similarly, in the post-Apartheid era in South Africa Manjoo (2005) recounts that South African Woman continue to be oppressed, particularly Black and Indian South African Women. While many Black South African men have had access to power, Black and Indian South African women for the most part still find themselves at the margins of the political and economic apparatus. Despite the effort of the African National Congress (ANC) to include women in the political body of the country, gender equality for South African women still remains a strongly desired goal to be achieved. As Manjoo (2005) observes:

> In theory the political commitment to gender equality and the advancement of women continue to exist ten years into democracy. Unfortunately, policies and commitment have not been effectively fulfilled in practice. It is clear that there is a range of challenges, at both the national and the provincial levels, in achieving the effective implementation of policies and commitments to achieve the goals of gender policy. (p. 4)

As the asymmetrical gender power relations in Nicaragua, Haiti, Algeria and South Africa reveals, it is clear that project of economic and political developments implemented in restern countries have mainly benefited men, especially men in privileged positions, but certainly not women. Given this situation, I believe that a political paradigmatic shift in these continents is urgently needed so that women can share the political and economic apparatus with men. Women have been oppressed for so long in Africa, in the Caribbean, in Latin America, and in many other parts of the world that a political victory or success of one or two women is always read and ideologically and politically constructed as an unprecedented historical event. This is evidenced in the "breaking and surprising news" about the two recently elected women in Liberia and Chile, Ellen Johnson-Sirleaf and Michelle Bachelet. This "breaking and surprising news" of these women's political victories clearly illustrates that women still have lots of steps left to take in the political ladder before they achieve equal political position with men. Until they achieve such a political position, their political success will most likely continue to be a surprise to this male dominated world.

All over the corporate mass media, the political victory of Ellen Johnson-Sirleaf and Michelle Bachelet was broadcasted worldwide. With the exception of the alternative TV and radio stations, such as *Democracy Now!* which problematized and critically analyzed this political event, most corporate mass media romanticized the presidency of these two women. Instead of seizing this crucial historical moment to challenge this unfairly and unevenly gendered world, extended European and U.S. media in the world overlooked the historical and political significance of the political victory of these two strong women. Unlike what was circulated through the mainstream mass media about the political victory of Ms. Johnson-Sirleaf and Bachelet, such a victory, in my view, casts light on the deferred human and political rights of restern women, human and political rights for which their female ancestors fought and died.

Despite all the lies we have been told in school (Loewen, 1995) through western hegemonic texts about the history of slavery and colonization we knew that enslaved and colonized women, such as Hariet Tubman and Milla Grandson, took active parts, just like enslaved and colonized men, in the arduous fight for their freedom and that of others. Like colonized and enslave men, many of them were tortured, murdered, and lynched for resisting the oppression of the European colonial system. Given female slaves' contributions to the end of slavery and colonization, one might have thought that the political victory of a descendant of African female slaves, like that of Ellen Johnson-Sirleaf in Liberia, would not surprise anyone. Unfortunately, that was not the case. Such a surprise about her victory clearly explains the sexist and patriarchal state we are still in. It also tells us that both men and women need to continuously fight to dismantle the patriarchal system that has been oppressive to women, especially women in the restern world.

Unquestionably, it is a real challenge for privileged African, Caribbean, Latin American, Asian men, and others, who have been in power for years, to be willing to battle against this sexist system, for such an action will go against their own male interest and privilege. However, this needs to be done because a life that is lived on the domination of others is voided of meaning. As much as men, out of fear, want to continue controlling women so they can stay in power, the time will come when they will have no other option but facing their fear. In order to transcend such a fear, which was invented and has been maintained by a capitalist and patriarchal society, men will have to establish what Foucault (1995/1977) called a self to self relation, rather than a self to the "other" relation, which places us in opposing and unequal power positions of a dominant subject and a dominate object. Similar to Foucault's to self to self relation is Paulo Freire's (1970) humanistic or, rather, revolutionary view about human relations. Freire (1970) maintained:

> One cannot be human when he prevents others from being so. Attempting to be more human, individualistically, leads to having more, egotistically, a form of dehumanization. Not that it is not fundamental to have in order to be

95

human. Precisely because it is necessary, some men's having must not be allowed to constitute an obstacle to others' having, must not consolidate the power of the former to crush the latter. (p.67)

What can be inferred from both Foucault and Freire's argument is that being human requires one to treat others humanly regardless of their gender and sex, race/ethnicity, social class, and nationality. This might seem a utopia in a world that is so gender-based to a point where one's gender predetermines what position she or he is expected to hold. Some people, however, have found ways to transcend this gender gate-keeping mechanism to fulfill their potential and influence the world political system. In the remaining of the chapter, I shall analyze the impoverished working conditions of women engendered by a western model of globalizations, then go on to challenge generalization and assumptions that have been made through research about the socio-economic and political situations of restern Women.

THE MORE THEY WORK, THE POORER THEY BECOME

This sentence above, in my view, reflects the socio-economic and working conditions of factory workers in the restern world. As transnational western capitalist corporations are closing their doors to workers in the West to settle in poor restern countries to maximize their profits, human rights activists more than ever are concerned about the rights of these factory workers. The inevitable question then becomes: who are these factory workers? If one were to pay a visit to these factories, or cared to find who numerically constitutes the labor force in these factories, one would quickly discover that it is predominantly women. This leads to further questions, such as: who are these women? What social class do they belong to? Any informed citizen of the world should not have trouble figuring out that it is poor restern women. One might, then, go on asking: how much money do these women earn per hour in these factories? Chomsky (1994), a linguist and a human right activist, casts some light on this question while describing the working condition of Haitian women factory workers:

> Baseballs are coming along nicely. They're produced in US-owned factories where the women who make them get 10 cents an hour-if they meet their quota. Since meeting the quota is virtually impossible, they actually make something like 5 cents an hour. Softballs from Haiti are advertised in the US as being unusually good because they're hand-dipped into some chemical that makes them hang together properly. The ads don't mention that the chemical the women hand-dip the balls into is toxic and that, as a result, the women don't last long at this work. (p. 78).

Chomsky's analysis of the plight of restern women casts light on how these women end up in this horrible working condition. However, one might wonder: How come they don't get out of this condition after realizing that they are being exploited and humiliated by the CEOs of the World Bank and the International Monetary fund? Restern women might be poor, one might say, but they are not so naive to the point that they don't know that they work long hours making Nike attire, thereby enriching their boss at their expense. Why is it, then, that poor Third Women do not break the cycle of poverty that these foreign corporate factories have engendered? Is it not their problem if they refuse to break that vicious cycle because, after all, they are the ones who are trapped in it? If one were to look at the situation of poor restern women factory workers from a Marxist standpoint, one would analyze it with a different eye interrogating the underlying reasons that led CEOs of these foreign factories to migrate to the restern world in the first place. One would find out that these CEOs moved there in search of cheaper labor and pose the following question: Why is there cheaper or, rather, the cheapest labor in the restern world? If one were from the restern world and had lived there long enough, like myself, one would most likely witness and experience the economic injustice to which restern countries have been subjected since their independence. One, therefore, will be in a better position to understand that it is not by accident that these poor female factory workers are trapped in the horrible working condition that they have been long found themselves in. One will then argue that the inhuman working conditions of restern women, who have been working in western-owned corporate factories, are more complicated than one realizes. Finally, one would arrive at this conclusion: restern women have been forced to work in those factories for survival because their countries have been economically and politically hijacked by the World Trade Organization (WTO), the International Monetary Fund (IMF), and the World Bank's (WB) economic policies, economic policies that have destroyed the economy of restern countries to a point that farmers could no longer continue doing their farming jobs to feed themselves and their families. Worse, such an economic policy has also widened the economic gap between men and women, as well as between underprivileged and privileged women in the restern world.

Although I was fortunate not to have to work in factories owned by western corporate factories, at the age of 14, I witnessed first hand the impoverished and inhuman economic conditions that family members and neighboors found themselves in while working in these factories. As a working class boy, I am reminded while visiting several times one my of female neighbors who was selling juice daily to factory workers at a factory located in my neighborhood. While sitting next to my neighbor who was selling juice to these factory workers who were predominantly women, I was able witness first hand their frustration and anger, and hear their complaints about their inhuman working conditions. Some of them complained that they did not get paid on time and, therefore, had to borrow money from neighbors to buy food and for transportation. Others were complaining not only about their poor salary but also about their male supervisors who were harassing them. My cousin, Joceline, (a pseudonyme) always complained about her male supervisor who wanted to sleep with her even though she told him that she was married.

Jocelyne never stop complaining about her back pain that she said was unbearable. At the factory where Jocelyne was selling her labor force, she was not allowed to speak with her co-workers who were mostly women. Factory workers, including Jocelyne, could only interact with their co-workers during the half hour lunchtime brake they were given. According to Jocelyne, the factory workers were

97

predominantly women. However, all the supervisors were men who often stood behind the workers making sure they were not talking to each other while working. In the words of Jocelyn, numerous times these supervisors reprimanded workers who were caught trying to talk their co-workers. Some of them were given written warnings, while others were threatened to be sent home without pay. If the workers needed something, they had to raise their hands, signaling it to their supervisors, who were usually right behind their back. Given the rigid restriction these female factory workers experienced, it can be argued that at these factories there was a climate of surveillance. By surveillance, I mean a set of hierarchical mechanisms put in place through these factories to control and normalize certain practices and subjugate others (Foucault, 1995/1977). The working conditions in and the rules that regulate the factory, where Jocelyne worked, fit Foucault's notion of surveillance in that they regulate and control daily practices, activities, and performance of Jocelyne and her female co-workers.

Maybe I was too young to understand that alienating labor could make workers feel exhausted, but what was not hard for me to comprehend was the constant complaint of my cousin about the horrible working conditions at the factory. Furthermore, what was not difficult either for me to understand was that Jocelyne left her house at 5:45 and did not come back until 7:00pm at night beaten with an exhausting looking face. The factory where Jocelyne worked, among others, was conveniently located near the Haiti's national airport. At first, I thought that was a coincidence that these factories were located less than five miles from this airport. Years later, I was able to understand the underlying reasons why they were located there. They were located close enough to the airport so that the raw products could easily be transported to these factories and the refined products produced by the factory workers could easily be shipped to the West.

Whoever does not understand the hidden agenda of those factories' owners to intentionally build these factories near a major airport, might hastily ask: What is wrong with the location of these factories? In other words, one might ask: Is there anything wrong with convenience? At first glance, one might also hastily agree that there is nothing wrong with the location of these factories. However, if one were aware of the massive migration of farmers to the capital of Haiti, Port-Au-Prince, that these factories caused, one would then understand why this convenient location for CEOs of these factories was an inconvenience to the country. There are multiple reasons that explain why the convenient location of these factories was indeed an inconvenience to Haiti. The first reason being poor farmers, who migrated to the capital in the hope of finding a job in these factories, ended up becoming an additional group of poor starving people after these factories were closed. As a result, the surrounding neighborhoods where these factories were located became overcrowded and overpopulated with poor peasants and farmers who left their rural areas to settle there. These factories workers, who were abandoned, left without jobs and consequently became beggars, prostitutes, and sometimes thieves in their neighborhood. Equally catastrophic, after the CEOs of these factories decided to leave the country for another country in search of much cheaper labor, the environment was greatly affected by the debris, the chemicals and polluting products left abandoned in these neighborhoods.

These are some of the pressing issues that seem to be overlooked by some western researchers who have conducted research on restern women. The economic, social, and political situations of restern women are complex and thus require critical ethnographic studies to understand them. Otherwise, one might run the risk of making erroneous assumptions about restern women living in the Caribbean, Africa, Asia, and Latin America. This has been the case in research conducted by western feminist researchers, such as Huston (1979) who, through her study, presented restern women's economic and political situations as if they are the same. In her study, Huston looked at the impact of the development process on the "family unit and its individuals members in countries such as Sri Lanka, Mexico, Sudan, Kenya, and Egypt" (Mohanty, 1986). She contended that concerns expressed by both urban and rural women workers in these countries revolved around education, access to health, training, work and wages, legal rights, and political participation. Thus, for Huston, as Mohanty (1986) noted, "the solution is simple: implement improved development policies that emphasize training for women field-workers; use women trainees and women rural development officers; encourage women's cooperatives; and so on" (Huston, pp.119-22, in Mohanty, p30). Such a generalization by Huston about restern women's complex lived experience requires one to ask the following question: Whose restern women's socio-economic and political situations the author is describing.

WHOSE RESTERN WOMEN'S LIFE?

Whose restern women's life? is a very important question to ask when one refers to restern women, who are not homogeneous. In the restern world, like in the western world, factors such as social class and race/ethnicity, are critically important to be taken into account in analyzing the struggles of women, as these factors shape and define their subjectivity. Being cognizant of the interrelation of these factors might help one avoid making generalizations and assumptions about restern women. Unfortunately, it has been quite common for westerners to generalize about the conditions of restern women. As historically documented, western researchers, including western feminist researchers, have often portrayed restern women in a way that denies the uniqueness of the experience of these women. These researchers have, through research, put restern women in similar-if not the same-categories. Reading the findings of these researches might convince one to believe that, for example, all restern women are religious, passive, obedient, and have experienced sexism with their husband the same say. This false and misleading image of restern women could explain the underlying reasons why many European male travelers have traveled to Asia, Africa, the Caribbean, and Latin America in search for docile and submissive women, as being portrayed through so-called empirical research.

The multiple human dimensions and complexity of restern women are often dismissed and shadowed in the narrowed, biased, stereotyped, and prejudiced analysis of western researchers about their lived experience. Because of a lack of an accurate picture of the complexity of lived experience of restern women, their political, social, and economic situations have not been truly known to the West. Worst of all, their resistance to fight the daily practices of sexism as well as the neoliberal and neocolonial effects of western economic and political policies on their material and spiritual beings has been overlooked. In short, they have been misrepresented by and in the West.

Furthermore, what is often lacking in some western-oriented research about the conditions of restern women is the clear link between sexism, classism, and racism that these women simultaneously experience. For example, as noted earlier, with globalization motivated by the western neoliberal economic agenda, the economic condition of restern women, particularly the poor ones, has gotten worse. Meanwhile, those who belong to upper class, including privileged restern Women, have gotten richer by exploiting poor restern women. Thus, analyzing the sexism that restern women have experienced without linking it, for example, to classism leaves space for doubt and suspicion. In other words, this might lead critical readers, who are reading findings of research conducted on restern women by western researchers, to ask the following questions: With what intention was this research done? Did it reflect the voices of restern women about their own living conditions? Or was it done to misrepresent and perpetuate stereotypes and prejudices about their political, socio-economic, and cultural situations? To simply put it, whose interests has this research served? Has it served the interest of restern women who often genuinely share their human, cultural, and historical resources with western researchers? Or has it served the academic interest of western researchers who appropriate the various resources of these women to further their own career and the western research academy as a whole? These questions are yet to be answered. As it has been documented, restern women, particularly the poor ones, have not benefited from research that has been conducted on them. If anything, they have for the most part been misrepresented through research conducted by western researchers, as evidenced in Huston's research.

In her breakthrough essay *Under Western Eyes: Feminist Practice*, Chandra Mohanty (1986) urged us to go beyond our stereotyped and prefabricated knowledge about the restern women in order to portray a fair and accurate picture of these women. Specifically, she encouraged us to challenge and reject the western homogenous political and cultural identities that have been imposed on restern women. Mohanty argued that some researchers, such as Huston, have portrayed restern women as if they have experienced sexism the same way regardless their social class, religious, social, and political locations. Challenging Huston's misleading and erroneous analysis about restern women, Mohanty (1986) contended:

> Huston assumes that all restern women have similar problems and needs. Thus, they must have similar interests and goals. However, the interests of urban, middle-class, educated Egyptian housewives, to take only one instance, could surely not be seen as being the same as those of their uneducated, poor maids. Development policies do not affect both groups of women in the same way. Practices that characterize women's status and roles vary according to class. (p. 30).

In challenging Huston's generalization about restern women, Mohanty provides us with a borderless critical language that allows us to understand the larger discussion about how some researchers tend to refer to a handful of either privileged or underprivileged restern women to draw a general conclusion about all restern women's economic, social, and political situations. This language also enables us to comprehend better the often distorted realities of restern women by the mass media, which usually draws upon, for example, the conditions of a few Sudanese, Somali, and Afghanistan women to generalize about women's lived experiences in the restern world.

Critically reflecting on Huston's generalization about the lived experience of restern women, I cannot help asking the following questions: How accurate can a representation of the "other" be when researchers document the interaction of their informants and collect and interpret data through their ideological lenses and their research agenda? Should one trust researchers' narration of others' stories when ultimately these researchers are the ones who decide what to keep or reject from the data they collected? Should one trust the image researchers portray of the people they study? In this regard, Peggy Phelan (1990) reminds us, "In doubting the authenticity of the image, one questions as well the veracity of she who makes and describes it" (p.1).

Moreover, given that one's bias, ideological position, and agenda often impact what and how one sees and analyzes social, cultural, and linguistic realities of others, shouldn't one then question researchers' textual production of their informants' narratives? As Atkinson (1990) contends, "The ethnographic text depends upon the plausibility of its account" (p.2). Decades ago, Said (1978) already warned us to be doubtful of texts, for they are not innocent. Constant questioning of texts might lead one to raise the concern as to why certain components of data are selectively chosen, prioritized, and saved while others are put aside and discounted. To problematize this further, I would question: How does the reader know if what truly reflects the lived experience of the informants does not get lost in this data selection? And how does the reader know the voices of the informants is not being truncated when ultimately researchers are the ones who decide consciously or unconsciously whose voices are valid or not?

Although researchers might have good intentions to narrate and represent as accurate as possible the doings and saying of their informants, the very language, as I argued in the previous chapter, they use to do so is not neutral. Language is loaded of ideology. Therefore its use, be it through oral and written texts, which are not value free, should be suspect, for it is often informed by one's interest and agenda. This might lead one to raise critical concern about how meaning is constructed. I must make clear that what is being articulated here about the use of language and meaning construction in research is not to promote cynical skepticism about research. Rather it is, at least for me, "to serve as a constant reminder that language and meaning do not exist in people's minds but in the multiple and interreletated set of discourses within which people are already situated" (Kamberellis & Dimitriadis, 2005, p.50).

While I still retain the hope that research can indeed offer the reader a detailed image of how life and culture are lived in certain communities and how knowledge is collectively constructed by people, I would, however, argue that it is critically important to question, challenge, and even deconstruct what researchers present to us as the "truth." The danger is that generally people believe in researchers and in their research findings. For instance, the belief that the researcher was "there" might convince the reader to believe what the researcher reports in his/her findings. My contention is that the belief that "a reality" is somehow "out there" waiting to be captured by researchers is too simplistic and could be misleading. The fact a researcher is "there" does not necessarily mean he/she will accurately capture "the reality" and/or will have access to the "truth." What researchers could offer the reader are partial truths, which should still be interrogated because their telling of others' stories might be partial and influenced by their biases, ideological position, and agenda. This is why representation, which is a key concept in both qualitative and quantitative research, needs to be clearly defined and understood by researchers before engaging in any research endeavor. The reason is that if representation of other people's stories, through research, is not carefully done, it can lead to their misrepresentation.

If research for the most part entails narration, construction, and presentation of the "truth" about people's stories, it should therefore challenge researchers to seriously think about the danger of "bestowing or disavowing the verisimilitudes of others" (Britzman in St. Pierre & Pillow, 2000). It should also challenge them to transcend their preconceived ideas, biases, and fixed agenda so they can capture the unthinkable, unforeseeable, and even undesirable that often emerge while doing a study. Given that research is expected to provide an accurate account about the "other's" stories, researchers therefore need to be fully aware of and cautious about how they textualize and present these stories to their targeted audience. To avoid misrepresentation, researchers need to be sure to ground as accurate as possible the narration of their informants' stories both in the words and the worlds of these informants. Hence, it is imperative that researchers ask themselves, if the written report of their research will do justice to their informants before publishing it. In other words, researchers need to ask themselves if their research report represents or misrepresents their informants' stories. The reason being that representation of others sometimes fails as a result of the way researchers use discourses to frame and analyze their informants' stories. When misrepresentation occurs, it inevitably leads lead to the truncation and fragmentation of the other's subjectivity. Given the challenge and intricacies involved in doing research, I propose that researchers question themselves and, if possible, find out if the people they claim to represent through their written text, if asked, would say that their stories are truncated and their subjectivities are fragmented. By failing to ask themselves such a question, researchers might end up presenting a truncated image of their informants.

Being of aware of this possibility, research critics such as Clifford (1986), have questioned and indeed rejected the belief that accurate representation of others is possible. Like Clifford, I am far from being convinced that accurate representation or the "whole truth" about resterners through research is possible, especially when western researchers enter the world of their restern informants with a colonizer's and "civilizator's" mind set. The reason is that the "truth" that researchers present about their restern informants is often-if not always-partial.

Thus, while I am not trying to be skeptical about the validity of research, I think the following questions need be asked before engaging in a study: What happens if the information the informant shares is what he/she suspects the researcher wants to hear? What impact would the informant's behavior have on the research findings if during the research she or he behaves and interact with the researcher in certain way to merely satisfy and meet researchers' curiosity, interest and agenda? And finally, what about if as a researcher what I think I see happening at the site is not what is actually happening? My contention is that researchers who deem these types of questions are crucially important to be asked might be better theoretically prepared to do quality research.

RESTERNERS' TRANSNATIONAL MIGRATION TO THE WEST

what is at stake?

We need to move beyond the antimulticultural, conservative ideology that claims, 'you immigrants came to our house for dinner and now you want to decide what's on the menu.' The reality for many is that we went into their homes and took more than we can ever give back.

Pepi Leistyna, Presence of Mind

These immigrants made bold and dangerous crossings, pushed by political events and economic hardships in their homelands and pulled by America's demand for labor as well as by their own dreams for a better life.

Ronald Takaki, A different Mirror

I speak in the name of the millions who live in ghettos because they have black skin or because they come from different cultures, and whose status is barely better than that of an animal. ...I speak out in the name of those thrown out of work by a system that is structurally unjust and periodically in crisis, whose only view of life is a reflection of that of the affluent.

Thomas Sankara, Thomas Sankara Speaks

People leave their native land to migrate to other lands for various reasons. Some voluntarily migrate to a foreign land to visit, study, and explore a different culture. International students, tourists, or travelers, especially those who are from western countries, fit that category. Generally, this category of people is not pushed by socio-economic and political circumstances to do so. Quite to the contrary, given their social class and country of origin, traveling frequently to other countries might be something they and their family do for enjoyment. Others, however, are forced to leave their country to seek a better life in a foreign land, as a result of unbearable religious and political persecutions and ethnic/tribal conflicts. Political, economic, and religious refugees fall into that category. Female prostitutes who, for economic reasons, are compelled to sell their body as commodities overseas, fit that category as well. Still others were forced to leave their lands after being captured and transported as commodities to alien lands. African slaves are a case in point.

In his studies on immigrants, John Ogbu (1998) broadly distinguished two types of immigrants, voluntary and involuntary immigrants. Ogbu classified African Americans as involuntary immigrants arguing that their ancestors were forcibly taken as slaves to foreign lands, such as the United States. In contrast, immigrants who were not shackled like the slaves while heading to a foreign land, are, according to Ogbu, voluntary immigrants. Although helpful, Ogbu's categorization of various types of immigrants is limited in that it fails to capture other crucial factors that led, or rather forced, people to leave their native land. As Leistyna (1999) notes," Contrary to researcher John Ogbu's idea of 'involuntary immigrants,' most groups do not come to the United States by choice. In fact, U.S. foreign policy, in places such as Latin America, Southeast Asia, Africa, and the Caribbean, has led to mass destruction and chaos, forcing people away from their homes" (p.26).

One of the fundamental factors that has constrained people, especially neocolonized people, to flee their land has been the harmful effect of the western neoliberal economic and political policies on the restern world. To be sure, the West, through globalization, which is the economic running machine of the World Bank (WB), the International Monetary Fund, the North American Free Trade Agreement, and the World Trade Organization, has economically and politically destroyed restern countries. These organizations have destroyed restern countries through unfair trade, by loaning them money with exorbitant interest rate, and by supporting the implantation of factories in these countries where the poor have been brutally exploited. As a result, many people, who have lived in these economically struggling and politically unstable neocolonized restern countries, have been forced to migrate, legally or illegally, to the United States, France, Spain, and Great Britain.

While the United States has been trying to block the entry of and repatriate a huge wave of "illegal" immigrants, France, Spain, and Great Britain have experienced an overwhelming flow of immigrants from Senegal and Ghana. Some of these immigrants have attempted to enter these imperialist countries under horrific conditions. For example, in their attempt to flee political chaos and poverty in their native countries, many African immigrants, particularly Senegalese immigrants, have tried to enter Spain by boat. While some have made it to these imperial lands alive, others have lost their lives.

Similarly, thousands of Mexican immigrants and immigrants from South and Central America have been trying to cross the United States/Mexico border under horrendous and dangerous conditions. Many have paid thousands of dollars to merely lose their lives and to be raped by their smugglers while trying to enter the United States, a country where many of these immigrants have been treated as second-class citizens. Worse, many of them have been chased and captured like animals in many states in the U.S., such as in California and in Texas.

These immigrants, like myself, who were forced to leave their country to migrate to western countries, such as the United States, are too often caught between two worlds: The West and the Rest. One world, the restern world, they dearly love and cherish but had to leave for socio-economic, political, and religious reasons.

This is also a restern world where generally these immigrants did not have to constantly worry about being discriminated against because of the way they look, the types of dress they wear, and the language they speak. Moreover, though impoverished because it has been exploited by the western world, it is a restern world where people are supported by their community in which an individual person matters to all of its members. Finally, this is a restern world wherein their cherished childhood and adult memories are rooted. Memories that suffocating forces of racism, linguicism, xenophobia, western ethnocentricism, and blind nationalism cannot ever and will never take away from them. In fact, I shall argue that the West, not even with its pointed guns and its biased legal system that often leads to unfair and unjustified incarceration of innocent people, cannot ever erase these memories. These memories not only sustain these immigrants morally and spiritually and help them maintain their human dignity, but they also empower and prepare them for unknown, unpredictable socio-political events or, better yet, movements. As Zinn (2003) eloquently put it, " The memory of oppressed people is one thing that cannot be taken away, and for such people, with such memories, revolt is always an inch below the surface" (p.443).

By contrast, the other world, the West, is a world where immigrants from the restern world have to cope with both overt and subtle racism and other forms of discrimination in institutions, such as in school, the work place, and the street. This is also a West where many immigrants are not genuinely appreciated enough for their contribution to its economic and political advancements and its military power. These immigrants have been used as political and economic objects by politicians and corporate institutions. Specifically, this is a western world where many of them who have become naturalized after years of struggle have been manipulated and used to elect candidates to various offices while they continue facing social, racial, and economic injustice. Worse, this is the same western world that has been sucking the resources of the restern world to which many of them feel they truly belong. Ironically, this is a western world, which many of them might prefer to the restern world and despite all forms of discriminations they daily have to fight against. Finally, this is a western world that has allowed many of them to say that they have a job in spite of their horrible working conditions—low pay and no benefits, such as health insurance, vacation, and sick pay. This is the dilemma many involuntary and voluntary immigrants have experienced living in the Diaspora.

As the negative effect of western neoliberal economic and political policies continues to impact poor people in the restern world, transnational migration of legal or illegal immigrants becomes an issue of great concern to many western countries and concerned citizens. In some countries, such as the U.S., Spain, France, and Great Britain, the arrival of legal and "illegal" immigrants has been at the center of political debates on national and foreign policies. For example, in 2006 the U.S. government attempted unsuccessfully to pass a bill into law, which would grant some "illegal" immigrants a work permit for a period of three years. In opposition to the provisions of that bill, millions of immigrants got on the street in May the same year protesting against it. Meanwhile, in France, after the unprecedented riot that took place in 2006 in some underprivileged neighborhoods where thousands of legal and "illegal" poor immigrants have lived, the French government took drastic legal measures to deport illegal immigrants who were involved in this riot. The riot, which caused damage to the economy of France, occurred as result of a poor immigrant of color who was unjustly killed by some French police officers.

The point that I am making by alluding to the struggles and dilemmas of restern immigrants who have tried to enter western countries is the following: As long as a western model of globalization continues to worsen the socio-economic and political situations of restern countries, western countries like the United States, Great Britain, France, and Spain will continuously face the massive migration of people coming from the restern world. If these western countries were serious about the immigration issue that seems to be getting out of their hands, they would first stop exploiting, through NAFTA, IMF, WTO, and WB, restern countries, such as Mexico, Haiti, El Savaldor, Nicaragua, India, Pakistan, and Afghanistan. Moreover, if they seriously want to solve the problem of "illegal" entry of immigrants to their territories, it is time they genuinely start to engage in a fair trade with restern countries, rather than trying to manipulate and control their political and economic systems. Equally important, if western countries do not want to have to erect fences by their borders to stop poor immigrants from coming in, it is time they show, not through words but deeds, that they respect the autonomy and sovereignty of restern countries. No country, I shall argue, be it poor and perceived as powerless, deserves to be economically and politically hijacked by western super powers. This, unfortunately, has been the case of countries, such as Haiti, Grenada, Panama, and more recently Iraq and Afghanistan that have been invaded and occupied by the United States and Great Britain.

FROM THE ISLAND TO THE MAINLAND: AN ODYSSEY

Like many involuntary immigrants living in the Diaspora, I have been caught between two worlds, the West and the Rest. Also, like those who were forced to flee their country, I was constrained to leave my native land Haiti primarily for political and economic reasons. I immigrated to the West in search of a "safer" and better life. I decided to come to the West after my older brother, who has resided there for five years, visited us in 1991 and strongly encouraged me to join him here, reassuring me that I would "make it."

Given the terror that paralyzed all of Haiti after the democratically elected president Jean Bertrand Aristide was ousted by the Haitian Yankee-army, I decided to follow my brother's advice and left the country a few years after he visited us. Like many immigrants, this was a huge decision that I made to immigrate to the U.S. because my dream had always been to stay in my country, work hard, and help others. However, such a dream had to be "deferred" (Hughes, 1965). I have lived in the West for twelve years, but I still wonder what happened to that dream, like Langston Hughes (1965) eloquently puts it in his poem, "A raisin in the Sun":

What happens to a dream deferred?
Does it dry up?
Like a raisin in the sun?

Or fester like a sore-
And then run?
Does it stink like rotten meat?
Or crust and sugar over-
Like a syrupy sweet?
Maybe it just sags like a heavy load.
Or does it explode?

Reflecting on my journey from a restern country to a western country, I now realize that my dream "sags like a heavy load," as Hughes stated. I have been carrying this heavy load on my shoulders for more than a decade now. Such a heavy load haunts me day and night, wherever I go and in whatever I do to "make it" like my brother said I would. This heavy burden haunts me because my desire to return to my native land diminishes daily. It diminishes because the country that I left behind in the 1990's is worse off now than it was then, despite its natural resources, beauty, and charm. Such beauty and charm glitter through its slow pace of life; its tropical and relaxing weather; its organic food and nice beaches; and the hospitability, generosity, and kindness of its people.

In spite of all these precious things that Haiti has to offer, my desire to return home is still decreasing because my home does not have enough windows of opportunities through which I can fly to help myself and others. The very few resources Haiti has, western imperialist countries, such as the United States and France, have stolen them. These resources have also been robbed by a very small but dominant group of Haitians who have been monopolizing political and economic apparatus of Haiti since its independence in 1804.

This dominant group, including the Haitian bourgeois and corrupt political leaders, has opted to work with and open all Haiti's economic and political doors to the U.S., France, and Canada to maintain the status quo. This is the same group, in cahoots with the Haitian Yankee-army, that has several times overthrown democratically elected presidents to protect their own interests and those of the western imperialist countries. Being disgusted by this situation, my desire to go back home in order to share my knowledge and skills with the younger generation is slowly dying. I fear that I might constitute a threat to the Haitian status quo that tends to favor mediocre intellectuals and professionals over those who are independent-minded, competent, and qualified.

Meanwhile, my life journey to the western world has been overcast by both bitter and sweet feelings. As noted earlier, living in the west after being forced to leave my native land feels like being caught between two worlds. On the one hand, I feel privileged to be in the West teaching at the college level while pursuing a doctoral degree. Living in the West has given me the opportunity to be exposed to multiple cultures and discourses that have widened my view of the world. Interacting with individuals from varying cultural, linguistic, and historical backgrounds has helped me become more open minded than before, accepting, and tolerant of others. This experience has also taught me that the world can be a better place if one gets out of one's skin to make an effort to socialize with and get to know the "other." Knowing the "other" might enable one to challenge old assumptions and learned stereotypes and prejudices that one holds against other people and cultures. In short, my experience living in the West has helped me become a more mature political, historical, and cultural being than I was twelve years ago.

On the other hand, like many involuntary immigrants, I feel trapped and some-times bitter living here in the West. I am bitter because I was forced to flee my country, which could have been politically and economically stable if it was not being exploited and destroyed by internal and external capitalist forces. I also am particularly embittered by a capitalist system which, via the corporate media, keeps feeding me the false hope and illusion that I can "make it" if I work hard enough. In fact, like millions of immigrants, since I immigrated to the West I have worked two jobs while going to school. For example, I was overworked and yet underpaid in multiple settings: (1) as a housekeeper and dishwasher in nursing homes and hotels where I spent long hours cleaning, sweeping floors and washing dishes; (2) as a valet hiker at a five star hotel where I had to park and retrieve fancy cars for the upper class western people; (3) as a case manager at a social service institution where I helped the elderly to meet their needs; and (4) as a Reading and ESL (Eng-lish as a second language) teacher who helped immigrant students learn the English language and improve their reading, writing, and critical thinking skills. But I still have not "made it"; I constantly have to manage life on a tight budget in order to make ends meet.

Similarly, other people of color, such as African Americans, Asians, Native Americans, Africans, and Latino/as, have been giving their sweat and blood to this system for decades, and yet the majority of them are still lagging in this "land of opportunity". One might wonder what excuse the dominant class uses to justify the too infrequent success of African Americans and Latino/as though success might not have meaning to those who have been marginalized by the capitalist system. Then the questions become: Have African Americans not worked hard enough giv-ing their blood for the independence and the economic stability of this country? How about the poor immigrants? Are they not overworked, underpaid, and ex-ploited picking strawberries in California, working long hours in factories, and fighting and dying in wars for the prosperity of this country and in the interest of the white conservative dominant class?

Given all lies that have been propagated via the corporate media about the West, it is imperative that the West be redefined. I suggest marginalized and oppressed groups, including restern immigrants, redefine it in their own terms, for they are the ones who, through the mainstream media, have mostly been lied to about the western model of democracy, meritocracy, and economic panacea. As demon-strated earlier in the book, the notion of western democracy and the so-called eco-nomic panacea still remain a dream, particularly for restern immigrants of color who constantly have had to fight against all forms of discrimination at work, in school, and in the street. If there is democracy and economic panacea in the west, they only work for western conservative dominant groups who have monopolized the wealth of the world for decades. However, for poor restern immigrants and other oppressed groups living in the West, western model of democracy has yet to be clearly defined and put into practice.

In the 1940's to 1990's communism was perceived as a real threat, and people of color were and still are considered a danger to the "civilized" and "democratic" western world. Lately it has been the religion of Islam and/or anyone who looks of Arabic descendants that are portrayed as a threat to the "civilized, democratic" western world. Ironically, western countries, which have portrayed themselves as tolerant and democratic, turn out to be intolerant towards individual self-expression, religious affiliations, and ideological differences. While the government of these countries takes pride in talking about freedom and democracy and try to export their model of these concepts to restern countries, its soldiers are violating people's human rights both in their backyard and abroad. The human rights of these people are usually violated based on their religious and political affiliations, national origin, or, as noted previously, merely because of the way they look, the type of dress they wear, the language they use to communicate with the word, and the god they believe in and worship. These have been the draconian actions taken by some western powerful countries in the name of democracy.

Besides the religion of Islam, slavery and colonialism are two dividing ingredients that have led to two diametrically opposing worlds: the West and the Rest. As it has been historically documented, the restern world as we know it today was a totally different world before the advent of slavery, colonialism, and the invention of racism by the white western conservative dominant class. During feudalism and the ancient Greece certain groups of people have surely known exploitation and oppression. However, the brutal economic exploitation and human subjugation that the poor in the Rest experienced during slavery and colonialism are unprecedented.

It is important to mention here that people in the restern world were not the only people and probably not the first ones who experienced slavery. As the prominent Haitian intellectual, Antenor Firmin (2000), notes, "The most superficial look into history teaches us that slavery has been a universal phenomenon that has existed in every country and in every race. There is not a single European people who has not known slavery at a certain stage in its history as a nation (pp.334-335)." In fact, as Firmin (2000) goes on to illustrate:

> In Western Europe, the institution by the Romans had the sanction of the law and remained part of the mores for quite a long time. Bristol, London, Lyon, and Rome each had a slave market where White bought their congeners and subjected them to the same regime they would later apply, but with a much more exquisite cruelty, to the Africans taken away from their native land thrown into a life of ignorance and utter abjection. (p. 335).

However, as Firmin points, the way Black slaves in the restern world experienced slavery was worse than the way western slaves in Bristol, London and Lyon experienced it. Clearly what differentiated a Black restern slave from a White western slave was their skin color. It can, therefore, be argued that the underlying reason that explains the cruelest treatment that Black restern slaves endured is racism.

There are other ethnic groups who have been victims of racism and other forms of discrimination similar to those of what the slaves had undergone. For example, under Hitler's dictatorship the Jews, the Gypsies, the disabled, and the homosexuals in Germany were victims of similar atrocity that the slaves endured during slavery. However, until, similarly, the human atrocity that Black experienced during slavery was inflicted on the innocent Jews, the disabled, the Gypsies, and the homosexuals by Hitler, the Europeans did not condemn it. They were silent about it and were even in complicity with it, for until then it was only inflicted on the slaves. The prominent Martiquese poet, Aime Cesaire (2000) fully captures the silent hypocrisy of the West about Nazism. Cesaire observes:

> ...that is Nazism, yes, but that before they were its victims, they were its accomplices; that they tolerated that Nazism before is was inflicted on them, that they absolved it, shut their eyes to it, legitimized it, because, until then, it had been applied only to non-Europeans people; that they have cultivated that Nazism, that they are responsible for it, and that before engulfing the whole edifice of Western, Christian civilization in its reddened waters, it oozes, seeps, and trickles from every crack. Yes, it would be worthwhile to study clinically, in detail, the steps taken by Hitler and Hitlerism and to reveal to the very distinguished, very humanistic, very Christian bourgeois of the twentieth century that without his being aware of it, he has a Hitler inside him, that Hitler inhabits him, that Hitler is his demon... (p. 36).

Hitlerism, I shall emphasize, was already taken place in similar form and shape during the slave trade and throughout slavery, but the Europeans chose not to speak against it. On the contrary, they closed their eyes on it so they could maximize their profits. Aligning with Cesaire's stance on Nazism, I would argue that Hitler's criminal and cruel act against the Jews and others was, in my view, a manifestation and a solid evidence of a deep-seated racism and the legacy of slavery that the west pioneered and inculcated in westerns' psyche. While the Holocaust must be strongly condemned and should never be repeated in world history, one ought to have, however, the courage to admit that it was indeed a call to the human consciousness of Westerners about human atrocity regardless on whomever it is inflicted.

IDEOLOGICALLY AND POLITICALLY NAÏVE, NO MORE!

Despite the influence of the corporate media, which has been trying to control my mind to make me believe that everything in the west is beautiful, I constantly have to remind myself of my past and present situations, so that I will not be caught up in my comfort zone here. I refuse to forget that there are millions of human beings like me, both in the western and in the restern world, that (1) do not have a place to live; (2) do not have access to clean and safe water; (3) are dying of hunger, diseases like AIDS, and curable diseases like tuberculosis; (4) are oppressed, tortured, and killed by their own governments, which are often supported by the West; (5) do not have access to basic literacy skills, such as being able to read the instruction of their medications (Kozol, 1966); and (6) have to move from city to city and from refugee camp to refugee camp to avoid the danger of losing their lives often caused by western inavasion and occupation, ethnic/tribal conflicts, and civil wars that are ravaging their countries. Sudan, particularly in Darfur, Iraq, and Afghanistan are cases in point. Finally, I have to humbly remind myself that there are people who have been dreaming for years to put their feet on the "land of opportunity and the free" for which the U.S. has dubiously earned a worldwide reputation. This is a land of opportunity and the free, however, where people have been marginalized and unjustly jailed due to their skin color, social class, linguistic backgrounds, and country of origin. Thus, I wonder who exactly has been benefiting in this land of opportunity and the free.

As a young boy growing up in a poor restern country like Haiti, I was brainwashed into believing that poor people are responsible for their own poverty, and that anyone can become rich if he or she works hard enough. In other words, I naively believed in what most conservative Americans believe in: meritocracy. What I failed to understand was that I was blaming the victims for their own victimization. I was not then fully cognizant of the fact that the unequal distribution of the world wealth, of which western imperialist countries have benefited, has been the main cause of poverty, hunger, and famine throughout the restern world. Nor was I keenly aware of how people could experience oppression, discrimination, sexism, homophobia, and xenophobia, because of their skin color, gender, [dis]ability, sexual orientation, social class, nationality, and religion.

My experience as a black restern immigrant living in the West has forced me to critically reflect on and question my politics, ideological, and social class locations, as well as those of others. Although one's racial and social class backgrounds can allow one certain privileges in society, I believe that these same backgrounds, placed in different political and socio-cultural context, can also be an obstacle to gain access to certain positions, particularly in a white male-dominated world like the western world. This leads me to be convinced that whiteness matters and is in itself a privilege. In fact, given the racist structure and infrastructure of some western countries such as the United States, England, Germany, Spain, and France, whiteness is equated to intelligence, bravery, calmness, beauty, and purity, while blackness is constructively equated to laziness, stupidity, savagery, anger, and ugliness. This is the type of white dominant ideology that institutions, such as schools, churches, and the media, have been propagating for centuries in order to keep certain racial and ethnic groups in marginal positions in society.

While growing up in the first independent black republic, I never knew what it means to be black and be treated as such. I first experienced blackness in the most brutally inhuman way here in the West. As a black restern immigrant, I have known all forms and shapes of racism living in the West. There have been times when the western world has almost made me feel ashamed of my racial identity, country of origin, and thus myself because of the way it has treated me. While sometimes I have felt invisible, other times I have felt really visible in the eyes of the western world. I felt and still feel visible when I am walking on the street and a white person fearfully and suddenly distances him or herself from me for fear of being robbed or physically attacked.

In *Black Skin White Mask*, Frantz Fanon (1967) recounted a similar experience he had in France with a white boy and his mother while walking in the street. The white boy, who evidently was scared of Fanon's blackness, fearfully called his mother while pointing to Fanon and said: "Look at the nigger!...Mama, a Negro!... Hell, he's getting mad...Take no notice, sir, he does not know that you are as civilized as we..." (p.113). Fanon (1967) analyzed this socio-racial injustice he experienced in the following terms:

> My body was given back to me sprawled out, distorted, recolored, clad in mourning in that white winter day. The Negro is an animal, the Negro is bad, the Negro is mean, the Negro is ugly; look, a nigger, it's cold, the nigger is shivering, the nigger is shivering because he is cold, the little boy is trembling because he is afraid of the nigger, the nigger is shivering with cold, that cold that goes through your bones, the handsome little boy is trembling because he thinks that the nigger is quivering with rage, the little white boy throws himself into his mother's arms: Mama, the nigger's going to eat me up. (pp. 113-114).

As Fanon's experience with the white boy and his mother illustrates, one's dark, brown or black skin tone often makes one a target. Moreover, depending on the context and geographical location, one's skin tone might make one visible or invisible. For instance, in Belchertown, located in the United States, particularly in the Western part of Massachusetts, I witnessed the nervousness and fear in my neighbors' face each time I opened the main entrance door to enter the building where I lived for about a year. The most "interesting" but frustrating experience that I had living there was when two of my neighbors completely ignored me when all I wanted to say to them was: "Good morning; how are you today." I was completely ignored as if I was an alien that invaded their "white western world." It did not take me long to realize that what scared them and pushed them away from me was not my genuine smile but my skin color which has nothing to do with my personality and humanity.

The attitude and action of some Belchertown police, who always followed me in my car to keep me in check day and night, confirmed the idea that in my neighbors' eyes and the Belchertown police's eyes I did not belong there. Moving from Belchertown to Amherst, Massachusetts, I thought that I would not continue being persecuted and followed by white restern police officers there; but it turned out that I experienced racism the same way as I experienced it in Belchertown. For example, I fooled myself believing that as a doctoral student living on campus I will be protected from racial profile, but what I failed to realize was that being a black restern student at the University of Massachusetts (Umass) at Amherst is not the same as being a white western student there. When I was in my car driving, my status as a doctoral student did not prevent a police officer from following me to keep me in check. From the constant attack and harassment of these white police officers, I soon realized that my black skin was the target and was, as the stereotype goes, the possible indicator that I might have carried drugs and gun in my car and /or be up to robbing and stealing. Hence, regardless of my personality, great ambition, and drive to pursue a higher degree to succeed, better my life, and contribute to society, I have to be kept in check simply because I happen to be one among the "dirty restern black immigrants" in some white police officers' eyes at Umass. Unlike white western students at this university I have to be extra cautious driving on campus and be mindful of the Umass Amherst police who might be on the corner waiting for me to make a little mistake to pull me over, drag me out of my car, and search it as if I was an illegal immigrant, a criminal.

Furthermore, I feel visible and fearful when I see millions of people of color are falsely accused for crimes they have not committed. I feel visible when I see people of color are being portrayed as drug dealers and gangsters in major Hollywood movies. I feel visible when I know millions of young Black and Latino men are incarcerated in jail where they continue enriching the capitalist class with their cheap labor. I feel visible when security guards keep staring at and following me as soon as I walk into stores, especially in stores located in "white neighborhoods." In a word, I feel visible because simply of my skin pigmentation, immigrant look, and foreign accent.

One the other hand, I feel invisible when, as an undergraduate student, three of my white professors ignored me in their class, which was predominantly white. I feel invisible when I do not see enough people of color in key positions, governmental or otherwise except a few "black puppets" who have been appointed governmental positions to merely fake racial diversity in the political apparatus of certain western countries. I feel invisible when black intellectuals and inventors do not receive enough appreciation and recognition for their contribution to the intellectual and scientific advancement of the world. Finally, I felt invisible when a secretary at a high school where I taught ignored me and refused to believe that I was teacher there while she acknowledged the presence of my white colleagues.

In spite of all, as expected of any individual I have tried to do "the right thing," that is, to be responsible, to work hard, and go to and stay in school. In other words, I have tried to be what is commonly defined as a "good citizen." However, this has not salvaged me from being seen and treated simply as a black man by the western world. Nor has it prevented western racist police officers from racially profiling and treating me as a subhuman. Since I immigrated to the West, I have felt that my racial and linguistic identities and human dignity have been constantly under attack. Realizing that despite all my achievements I have been still treated simply as a black man I decided to use my inner strength and confidence to affirm my blackness and lift it up as high as possible. However, the western world has still found ways to make me feel ashamed of my blackness by associating it with derogatory terms, such as "black market" and "black box" and phrases like "don't blackmail me."

Although I have tried to better understand the western world by assimilating into it, it still has treated me like an outsider. I have attended the same school as the western man and woman in the western world; we have lived in the same neighborhood; taken the same airplane and public transportation; gone to the same club to party and drink together; worked together and had dinner to the same restaurant; drunk the same water and breathed the same air; listened sometimes to the same music; and watched basketball, football, and baseball together, yet the western world remains an unknown world to me. It is like a closed gate that I cannot break through despite my academic achievement, level of intelligence, and good manner. I have tried diplomacy, kindness, and politeness, hoping that I will be welcome in the western world, yet I still feel unwelcome and, paradoxically, caught in it.

Like other restern immigrants of color, this western world has congratulated me on my academic and professional accomplishments; however, it still questions my humanity. Because I just happen to be different in the eyes of this western world, it has refused to see and treat me as a human being. Instead, it has merely treated me as black refusing to go beyond my blackness to see and treat me as a whole person. This racial injustice, of which I have been a victim in this western world, is brilliantly captured by Fanon (1967), who agues "As color is the most obvious outward manifestation of race it has been made the criterion by which men are judged, irrespective of their social or educational attainments."

On many occasions, I decided to protest against the outsider status that has been unfairly assigned to me in the western world. I have protested, arguing that I have no control over my birth, blackness, and country of origin. Further, in my protest, I have stated that I do not deserve to continue to carry the burden of slavery that my ancestors brutally endured. I have also asserted that, like every human being, I can only learn from and connect to the past, live in and shape the present, and help build the future. All of this, however, has not gotten me far in regaining my human rights that have been violated on countless occasions by the western world. Repeatedly, the western world has tried to murder my voice. I have fought back asserting that, "voice is a human right. It is a democratic right" (Macedo, 1994). However, my assertiveness has not helped me much in my battle for reappropriating my human dignity. Thus, I concluded that, no matter how knowledgeable an educated restern person of color is, she or he most likely will not be taken seriously by the western world, which foolishly and blindly still believes that it is superior to the restern world.

In this regard, it is worth alluding here once more to Frantz Fanon's stance against what I would call raciality in *Black Skin White Mask*. Narrating his experience as a black immigrant living in France, Fanon (1967) states, "I am given no chance. I am overwhelmed from without. I am the slave not of the "idea" that others have of me but of my own appearance." Fanon's experience with racism in France is quite similar to that of many restern immigrants color, including myself, who in most cases involuntarily immigrated to the Unites States. As I have experienced xenophobia and racism here in the west, the message coming from the western world has become clearer to me: if you do not look like us, do not sound like us, therefore you cannot be a part of us. Like Fanon, "all I wanted was to be a man among other men." But the western world has denied me my manhood and, worse, my humanwood because of my racial, linguistic, and cultural differences. As a counter strategic resistance to the ill treatment that I have repeatedly received from the western world, I decided, like million of "postcolonial" subjects living in the Diaspora, to resort to my inner-self to reconnect with and fully accept myself, rather than hanging around and waiting for the western world to accept me and who I am, which is a reflection of my racial, cultural, linguistic, sexual, and socio-political identities which, under no circumstances, I will compromise.

THE REST INSIDE THE WEST

Haiti vs. New Orleans during katrina

We are ugly, but we are here.

Edwidge Danticat

During the Katrina tragedy, which devastated New Orleans and uprooted thousands of people, several American commentators were invited by many television stations to comment on such a horrible catastrophe. One of the invited commentators said something along those lines: *Is this the United States of America? These images remind me of Haiti. This is not acceptable.* Like any public intellectual, I was concerned that such a comment, if taken at face value, would simply perpetuate even further stereotypes about restern countries, while failing to capture and interrogate the conspiracy that western countries, including the U.S., have been plotting against poor African Americans, poor immigrants, and poor white folks who were abandoned during Katrina. My goal in this chapter is not to merely analyze the comparison that the commentator made between New Orleans and Haiti during Katrina. I shall problematize and link his comment, on a larger global scale, to exploitative conditions, stigmas, and stereotypes to which both poor people in the western and the restern world have been subjected.

Referring to the statement above, one would probably infer that all the looting, ugly, and starving faces during Katrina reminded the American commentator of Haiti, but not the United States of America. What happened in New Orleans is not acceptable, but it is or will be acceptable in Haiti. In other words, whatever is ugly reminds one of poverty, or the destruction of one's property symbolizes Haiti. What the American commentator stated virtually spoke to power, but it was stated in a very naïve and condescending way. It is true what happened in the street of New Orleans during Katrina somewhat reflected what has been happening in Haiti and in other parts of the restern world.

Like in New Orleans during Katrina, in Haiti people usually get on the street and loot whenever there is political and economic turmoil. They illegally enter stores seeking food or whatever they can get to cloth and feed themselves and their family. During political and economic instability, the starving poor and exploited Haitians usually target stores owned by the Haitian bourgeois, who has been exploiting them for decades. In short, the disinherited Haitians never miss the opportunity to loot when the political and economic situations of Haiti get out of control. Should their looting actions and those of African Americans and some poor White people in New Orleans during Katrina be justified? The answer is evidently, no.

But can and should it be understood? I would say, yes. How can one then understand and explain what led people in New Orleans and in Haiti to loot during Katrina and during political and economic disturbances in Haiti? I would argue that in order to arrive to a better understanding of what recently happened in New Orleans and what has been happening in Haiti, one needs to question the political and socio-economic system of the western world and how it has negatively impacted poor people both in the western and the restern world. By simply arguing that, New Orleans is not Haiti, this commentator only perpetuates the stigma about the first Black independent nation that the West has been putting under its economic, political, and cultural siege for decades. Such a statement does not speak to the core and the roots of the economic, social, and political problems that New Orleans and other restern nations, such as Haiti, have been facing for decades. Instead, it "otherizes" another poor nation that has been fighting for social, economic, and political justice like poor people in New Orleans.

Moreover, such a statement does not show any compassion and respect for a black nation that fought against slavery and colonialism, and has been fighting since its independence against western neocolonialism. Nor does it show any support to the daily struggle of poor people regardless of their geographic and cultural locations. In short, such a statement seems to send the following message: we might be black and poor, but we are not like the Haitians who are part of the restern world. Obviously, the commentator failed to realize that the restern world has been existing within the western world for centuries. The American's comment, in my view, is a discourse of cold distancing and dissociation from the "other." Such a discourse is empty of compassion, love, and solidarity with humankind. Challenging his comment, I would assert that he grossly failed to understand that the war of poverty that corporate western governments have been perpetrating against poor people does not exempt any of them, whether they are living in the western or in the restern world.

Katrina could have been used as a critical historical moment to unveil and question a hegemonic, racist, capitalist, ableist, and sexist system that has marginalized poor black, poor white, elderly, and poor people with disabilities. What occurred in New Orleans during Katrina could also have been used as a political and ideological tool to galvanize a mass movement like the ones that took place in the U.S. and in Africa in the 60's against racism, colonialism, and Apartheid. Simply put, this human tragedy could have been wisely used as a political and ideological weapon to promote political and social awareness among people of color within the U.S. and abroad. Equally important, Katrina could have been used as an opportunity to launch a campaign against sexism given lots of poor elderly women, pregnant women, and women with small babies were neglected and lost their lives during this tragedy. In brief, this commentator, who condescendingly compared the devastated New Orleans to Haiti, missed a great opportunity to directly attack four evils that have negatively impacted not only New Orleans but also the entire world, of which New Orleans is a part. These evils are ableism, racism, sexism, and capitalism.

I wish to briefly talk about these four isms situating my analysis in the New Orleans context and, on a broader scale, the U.S. context. I shall begin with ableism. During Katrina, there were many people with disabilities who lost their lives due to the carelessness of a system that has historically valued able-bodied people over those with disabilities, particularly poor people with disabilities. Perhaps it will never be known how many poor blind, deaf, bed-bound people, and people with other types of disability lost their lives during Katrina. They were treated as if their life did not matter as much as the life of rich people whom family members and/or the government rescued. This was even worse for poor black people with disabilities because, besides their disability, they had another ism that played against them, racism.

Like South Africa, the U.S. is well known worldwide for its history of exploiting, mistreating, and isolating people of color. Since slavery until now, people of color in the U.S. have been neglected and exploited by the US white dominant class despite their tremendous contribution to the economy of this country. They have contributed to the economy of this country by working for pennies while being in jail; they have strengthened the U.S. economy by working in factories under horrible working conditions. Finally, they have made the U.S. economy stronger by being sent to and dying in wars that have strengthened the U.S. economy. Here I am referring to wars that the U.S. got involved in and used as a political and economic tool to exploit resources of nations that it has bombarded, invaded, and occupied.

It is undeniable that people of color in this country continue being the victim of the legacy of slavery, and the Katrina tragedy clearly confirms it. If the New Orleans tragedy had occurred in a state in the U.S. that is predominantly white, like New Hampshire or Vermont, I wonder how the U.S. government would have responded. Would it have waited for thousands of people to die before sending soldiers/police and other forces in the army to "rescue and save" them? If the face of people living in New Orleans were white faces, would the U.S. government have been reluctant to financially help the destroyed poor black families to get back to their hometown and start over a normal life? These are the questions that I believe should be at the core of discussions about the aftermath of Katrina, rather than stigmatizing a poor but a proud and historically glorious country like Haiti. I also believe that these questions need to be answered, as opposed to being silent about them or superficially talking about them.

Katrina also brought to the forefront the gender question, precisely the gendered unequal power relations that constitute the very fabric of the U.S. economic and political system. It is unquestionable that people of color have been exploited, but I believe that women of color have been victims of exploitation to a greater extent than men of color due to sexism. Again, Katrina confirmed this assertion when, for example, thousands of elderly and poor black mothers were left dying in their flooded home without any serious attempt from the U.S. government to rescue them. As it was reported during and after the tragedy, lots of black mothers lost their lives while they were trying to save the lives of their children. Poor elderly women were left abandoned in hospitals and in their house while helicopters were

rescuing able-bodied men, particularly white men. To further this argument, however, it must be noted here that white women have also been facing sexism, especially the poor ones. But for women of color it has been even more challenging
because of the intersection between racism and sexism. Furthermore, capitalism,
which generally affects people regardless of their race and skin tone, affects
women of color to a much greater extent than white women.

The Katrina tragedy makes it clear that any analysis of capitalism requires one
to include the social class component of it. As a capitalist country, the U.S. is divided into poor working class, middle class, upper middle class, and upper class.
This became evident during the Katrina catastrophe. Regardless of the mass media's attempt to conceal the truth, the informed public came to the realization that it
was mainly the privileged black and white people who were able to quickly escape
and safely survive the tragedy in New Orleans. The poor black and white did not
have the means to quickly leave New Orleans and relocate themselves somewhere
else before the hurricane destroyed their house and family. Nor did they have the
economic capital to return to New Orleans a few months after the tragedy to re-
build their houses that were destroyed. Quite to the contrary, hundreds of poor
black people and a fair number of poor white, who landed, for example, in Hous-
ton, Texas, were being piled up like poor political and economic refugees in stadi-
ums. They were treated like poor refugees in their own land, which has ironically
been called a land of opportunity.

During the tragedy, the mass media only portrayed people of color who were
waving flags, while standing on the roof of some houses to make themselves visible to rescuers, who ignored many of them. Lots of poor people of color and white
people were perished while their lives could have been easily saved. Despite the
images of these poor black families that were repeatedly shown on the U.S. major
TV channels, such as Fox news, CNN, and NBC, the informed citizens knew that it
was not only them who were in these horrible situations; they knew that there were
poor white folks who also were trying to escape the tragedy but did not survive it
because of their social class. Furthermore, in spite of the fact that the mass corporate media tried tirelessly to portray people of color as thieves and looters, we also
knew that there were some poor white who were also involved in looting. They
simply were not portrayed on TV like people of color.

Though horrible, what happened in New Orleans is a perfect example of the
intersectional relation between restern and western nations, race, class, gender, and
disability. Drawing upon the economic and political dimensions of what happened
in New Orleans, I would contend that Katrina has finally forced people to admit
that the restern world, which has been negatively portrayed and exploited at the
same time by the western world, also exists within the U.S. My argument is that
the only difference is that the restern world within the U.S. is composed mainly of
poor Black, Latino/a, Asians, White, and other poor ethnic groups. The other restern world outside the U.S., on the other hand, is mainly made of poor people in
poor countries that were formerly colonized and continue being under the western
economic, political, and cultural dominations.

The human tragedy in New Orleans makes it quite clear that the legacy of slavery and colonialism still drastically impacts people of color. In fact, I would argue that what happened in New Orleans is a direct consequence of internal neocolonialism in certain parts of the U.S. Neocolonialism is not a economic and political monster that only haunts people living in restern countries. Marginalized groups of African or Caribbean descendants living in imperialist countries, such as Great Britain, France, and the U.S., also have to fight against neocolonialism within these countries. From this analysis it follows that, regardless of where "postcolonial" subjects are geographically relocated, they will continue to be victimized by the negative consequence of the economic and political policies of western neocolonial and imperialist countries.

Hence, it is important that one goes beyond the western border to analyze the question of race, nation and state, and class at a global level. Instead of trying to rescue New Orleans from the stigmatized Haiti, one could have problematized and critically analyzed what happened in the city of New Orleans. In other words, in comparing Haiti to Katrina, one could have, for example, questioned why Haiti is so poor. This question would have led one to interrogate the imperial attitude and action of the U.S. and France against Haiti and other poor restern nations. Furthermore, using the situation in New Orleans as a political framework, one could have talked about U.S. imperialism and its indifference towards poor people, whether they happen to be poor African Americans, Latino/as, Asians, Native Americans living in New Orleans or other poor people living in the restern world. Finally, since New Orleans is predominantly inhabited by people of color and located in the richest country of the world, one could have used it as a departure point to mobilize and raise racial and political consciousness among people of color throughout the world. Simply comparing what happened in the street of New Orleans to Haiti did not further the political debate toward possible answers to the questions of racism, classism, sexism, ableism, inter-neocolonialism, and neoliberalism from which both people in New Orleans and in the restern world have suffered. Nor did it challenge the U.S. government to assume its responsibility towards African Americans who lost their lives and became homeless as a result of Katrina.

Unlike what the U.S. senator Barack Obama stated in his speech during the democratic convention in 2004 in Boston, Massachusetts, what happened in New Orleans once again reminds us that there is not one United States of America. In his speech, Obama said:

> Now even as we speak, there are those who are preparing to divide us, the spin masters and negative ad peddlers who embrace the politics of anything goes. Well, I say to them tonight, there's not a liberal America and a conservative America; there's the United States of America. There's not a black America and white America and Latino America and Asian America; there's the United States of America. (p. 2).

Such a statement, in my view, is dishonest and misleading and consequently can lead to the perpetuation of lies embedded in the "color blindness notion," which some privileged white people have purposely used to maintain the status quo.

These privileged white people have used "color blindness" as alibi to claim that they are not racist, arguing that they treat people of color based on who they are but not on their phenotypes. While they state that they are not racist, they continue to take part in maintaining and benefiting from the racist system that oppresses people of color, rather than striving to change it.

Senator Obama's statement also shows a great level of disrespect to African Americans, Native Americans, Asians, Blacks, and Latinos/as who have been singled out and marginalized due to racism and white supremacy in this country. Moreover, his statement seemed merely intended to please the white conservative dominant class who, throughout history, has been stigmatizing, stereotyping, and exploiting people of color, including the Senator. Finally, such a statement spoke against the Senator himself whose white side has been shadowed and even denied by such a racist society. As Mr. Obama knows or should know, the United States of America has historically been denying people's biracial identity by simply putting them in "one Black, Philipino/a, Asian, Latino/a box" and thereby completely disregarding their other side(s). In the case of people who are half white and half black, their white side has always been historically, legally, and socially denied for specific reasons. One of which has been to prevent them from having access to political, economic, and social privileges that are attached with whiteness in the world.

Perhaps Senator Obama made such an unfair and incorrect statement because as a child, who was raised by a white middle class mother, he was able to have access to some kinds of white privilege. Had Mr. Obama been raised by his immigrant Kenyan father, I wonder how his experience as a mixed child would have been in this country? Has not Obama been targeted in the street, in stores, and racially profiled by white racist police officers in this country regardless of his biracial identity? As the columnist, Leonard Pitts (2006), notes:

> Assume for a minute Obama didn't have a famous face. Assume he was just another brother tooling down Main Street. Do you really think the cop who pulls him over for no good reason is going to change his tune if he is told Obama's mama is white? 'Oh. Sorry, Mr. Obama. I didn't realize you were BIRACIAL. Have a good day.' No way. You may be many things, but if one of them is black, that trumps the rest in terms of how the world sees you. Black is definitive.

The tragedy in New Orleans clearly demystifies the dishonesty and falsehood in Mr. Obama's statement. Contrary to what Obama said in his speech, Katrina proves that there are in fact a white America, a black America, a Latino/a America, and an Asian America. To paraphrase what the former American president Jimmy Carter said in his speech delivered during the funeral of Martin Luther King's wife, the tragic event of Katrina is a convincing fact that the United States is still racially segregated. I would add that Katrina has proven that the U.S. is far from being a country where people of color will ever be on an equal economic footing with white people.

Going back to the comparison that was made between Haiti and New Orleans as a result of Katrina, I would state that it is sad that Katrina had to be the tragic event that stirred up many people in this country to realize that there is indeed a restern world within the borders of the western world, namely the United States. The existing restern world in the U.S. has simply been denied and concealed by those in powerful positions. As previously noted, the irony of all this, though, is that the U.S. is considered the most prosperous country of the world, while millions of its people are starving, do not have access to health care, and, worse of all, are homeless like millions of people in the restern world. The questions then become: Who has been benefiting of the wealth of the United States? Specifically who has been profiting the wealth that the United Stated has accumulated throughout the years by invading, occupying, and exploiting other countries in Africa, in the Caribbean, in Asia, South/Central America, and in the Arab world?

There are many historical lessons that can be learned from Katrina, which forced many poor black families to scatter all over the United States like the slaves during the slave trade. Three of these lessons are fundamental. First, what happened in New Orleans clearly showed that racism is still deeply rooted in the fabric of American society despite the civil rights movement that opened some doors of opportunities to some people of African descent in this country. However, these doors of opportunities that the civil rights movement has opened to a few people of color have not changed the fact that the U.S. state apparatus has been mainly serving the interest of the white dominant class. Second, Katrina has taught us or should have taught us what is happening locally should be linked to what happens globally, for the local informs the global and vice versa. To situate this argument in the context of New Orleans and Haiti, I would contend that the Katrina tragedy represents a challenge for African Americans-- especially for those who tend to be blind nationalist and thus run the risk of holding a provincial view on racial and social class issues-- to look at the struggle of black people beyond the U.S. border. Third, this tragedy challenges or should have challenged us to be sensitive to and help fight against the horrible economic plight of restern nations, such as Haiti, Somalia, Liberia, Sudan, and Rwanda, instead of contributing to perpetuate the negative image that the U.S. mass media has already portrayed of them. My contention is that any battle aimed to end poverty and fight negative stereotypes against poor people must be global; it should not simply be national or local. As previously noted, Katrina most importantly brings to the fore the undeniable fact that the restern world is located inside the western world though in a subtle way. Finally, Katrina illuminates the intersection of race, class, gender, and disability and how this intersection impacts all of us regardless of our ideological and political locations in the world. Simply stated, one cannot and should not talk about race without linking it to gender, class, and disability issues; nor can one do a serious critical analysis of class without connecting it to race, gender, and disability, for we are all living in a racialized, gendered, and social class-based society. There is no way to escape this interconnected triangle because it constitutes our embodiment as political, cultural, spiritual, and human subjects.

Ending this chapter, I would reiterate that it cannot and should not be denied that the image that the mass media portrayed of New Orleans during Katrina did, in fact, somewhat reflect what has been happening in some restern countries. However, one needs to go beyond such a biased and racially motivated image to unveil the deep economic and political problems both New Orleans and many countries in the restern world have been facing. Trying to save the face of New Orleans by stating that it is not in the same ugly, poor, horrible economic, and political conditions as Haiti does not point to the core of the economic and racial problems that have negatively impacted such a beautiful city. Such an approach simply offers a superficial analysis of environmental, political, and economic factors that led to the Katrina tragedy, while it belittles Haiti, the island from which many black folks in New Orleans originated. Katrina has offered a great opportunity to American political analysts to unmask and speak against, on a global scale, the deep racial, economic, and political divide between privileged and poor people as well as between western and restern nations. Unfortunately, the commentator did not seize such a noble opportunity to speak back to the western imperial power, such as the United States, that has neglected and exploited poor people in its back yard and abroad.

GOING BEYOND

For us, the problem is not to make a utopian and sterile attempt to repeat the past, but to go beyond. It is not a dead society that we want to revive. We leave that to those who go in for exoticism. Nor is it the present colonial society that we wish to prolong, the most putrid carrion that ever rotted under the sun. It is a new society that we must create, with the help of all our brother slaves, a society rich with all the productive power of modern times, warm with all the fraternity of olden days.

Aime Cesaire, Discourse on Colonialism

My final prayer:

O my body, make of me always a man who questions!

Frantz Fanon, Black Skin, White Masks

To paraphrase Aime Cesair, in talking throughout this book about colonialism and neocolonialsim it is not a dead society that I want to revitalize, nor is it the current neocolonial western empire that I wish to prolong. Instead, by doing so my aim is to help both resterners and westerners to better understand the negative impacts colonialism and neocolonialism have had on the educational, socioeconomic, cultural, and political structures of both the restern and the western worlds. Moreover, by sharing my lived experience and knowledge about western neocolonialism and neoliberalism with people living both in the West and in the Rest, I hope that I fulfilled my responsibility as an educator. This type of knowledge has often been concealed from marginalized groups by the dominant class in society. Indeed, dominant groups have often prevented dominate groups from having access to certain sociohistorical facts because allowing the latter to have access to these facts might constitute a menace to their interests. This explains why information is such a powerful tool, especially when individuals can take any information to analyze it, contextualize it, and try to link it to their daily life realities or experiences.

Furthermore, in speaking against the disastrous effects of neoliberalism, neocolonialism, linguicism, and sexism on people both in the western and the restern worlds, my goal is to help the reader discover alternative ways to combat these ism so that collectively they can imagine and attempt to build a new world. A new world where educational, social, political, economic, and gender justice and equalities will no longer be a dream, and which will be governed by principles and rules whereby every country should be bound regardless of the country's hegemonic political and economic influences on the world. These rules and principles, which every country should obey and follow, should consist of equal access to a quality education for all, fair trade between nations, and equal redistribution of the wealth of the world between the West and the Rest. Does such a proposal sound too ambitious, too demanding, or simply too revolutionary? I am certain that many privileged people both in restern and western countries might argue that it is indeed too revolutionary, as a real and true revolution is the enemy of their corporate economic and political interests.

Suppose that my ambitious proposal sounded too threatening to some dominant groups or countries, what are other options for a livable or a more livable world would we then be left with? Are we going to continue to live in a world where the school system is used as a laboratory where students' young mind is ideologically and carefully programmed in a way that prepares them to reproduce inequalities from which marginalized groups have suffered? Are we going to accept to continue to live in a world where the education one receives does not empower one to interrogate the world, like Frantz Fanon's wish suggested, and attempt to change one's socioeconomic, cultural, and political conditions? Or are we hoping that our students will be taught in school individualistic navigation skills so they can navigate through the system and make millions out of it at the expense of others? Or rather, are we hoping that they will be taught in school how to intelligently position themselves within the system to understand it, question it, and try to transform it? Are we willing to continuously send our children to a school system that is still colonial-based? Or are we going to strive to change it? As educators, are we going to continue to emulate old colonial teaching practices and methods that were passed on to servant teachers who worked to maintain the colonial school system?

With regard to western neoliberalism, are we going to allow powerful western countries to make us believe that the World Bank, the North American Trade Agreement, the World Trade Organization, and the International Monetary Fund are the hope of the restern world? Or are we going to take political stance to clearly tell the West that we have witnessed what these organizations have done to poor men, women, and children both in the restern and the western worlds? Stated otherwise, are we going to find ways to inform the entire world that these organizations have further impoverished the poor who are working under horrible working conditions in U.S. owned factories located in the restern world? Are we going to inform citizens of the world about agricultural products produced by farmers that have been devalued due to cheaper imported products from the western world?

Furthermore, are we going to inform our students and our own children about the harmful effects of western model of globalization on people in the restern world? Or are we going to misinform them by telling them that western globalization is the panacea to their socioeconomic and political problems? Are we going to encourage them to emigrate to the West, while failing to inform them that immigrants, legal or "illegal," living in western countries have been discriminated against, brutally exploited, illegally detained, and treated as sub-humans? Are we going to help them understand what causes the restern world to be economically and politically stagnant, unstable, and dependent, and what causes transnational migration of resterners to the western world? In short, as educators, activists or simply as responsible citizens, are we going to continue to live in the fearful state we have been put in? Or are we going to try to find ways to go beyond our fear to live courageously and truthfully and help our students and children become ambassadors of truth, rather than perpetuators and spokespersons of lies?

Obviously, one's answers to these questions posed above will vary depending on what side of the ideological and political battles one chooses to be. For educators who feel that they have a moral and an intellectual obligation to educate and inform their students, they need to interrogate what they have been told and sold as the truth. It is only through constant interrogation can we make sense of "the truth" that we have been told and then come up with our own version of it. Moreover, it is crucial to question because it is through questioning we might be able to unveil lies that have been circulated through the school materials we are required to use to teach, and educational policies we abide to follow. These lies also get circulated through our living rooms where our TV set is located; through work places where we sell our physical and intellectual labor; through places where we socialize; and even through church which we attend every Sunday or quite regularly.

In this age of neoliberalism, alternative strategies that I have proposed throughout the book to counter and resist the horrendous effects of colonialism and neocolonialism on the educational, socioeconomic, and political structures of restern countries might seem in the eyes of many unrealistic strategies. If that is the case, I will understand for I am fully aware that we are all living in a world that is controlled by a mass corporate media, which has incessantly tried to control people's mind and make them believe a certain version of truth about the world; a version of truth that only serves the interests of the dominant class. The media in itself is a neutral medium of communication. It is corporate organizations like Disney, Coca Cola, and Wall Mart that own and control the media and transform it into a tool that serves their interests. Unfortunately, people, including educators who lack political consciousness, have been conditioned to consume and believe ideas that the media has been selling them. People's consumption of misinformation spread by the corporate mass media is an educational issue that should concern us all as educators.

Do these suggestions above sound revolutionary, too? Whether they do or do not, triggering a revolution of novel and transformative ideas for social change in the mind of their students is something that all progressive educators should strive for unless they lose sight of what should be the ultimate goal of education. The ultimate goal of education, in my view, should be about co-constructing knowledge with students and encouraging them to critically use acquired knowledge to first revolutionize their mind and then try to effect social change. I do not believe people can or help effect social change unless they first revolutionize their mind, which might have been conditioned to think in way that refuses to open itself up to social change. Thus, by attempting to know how ideas, values, and beliefs, which have been inculcated in their mind since kindergarten, influence how they perceive the world, students will develop self awareness, which they can use to first change their old ways of thinking so that they can contribute to educational, socioeconomic, and political changes. My contention is that self awareness is key and conducive to any type of change, be it personal change and/or social change. In fact, I would go further arguing that having access to any type of knowledge without self awareness can be destructive because, as Michael Eric Dyson (2004) brilliantly put it, "Knowledge, after all, is not neutral, neither the getting of it nor the keeping of it, or even the uses of it. Besides the pleasures it brings, knowledge can also be dangerous, subversive, and liberating" (p. xxiv).

Expanding on Dyson's argument, I would assert that it is crucial that we continuously question and deconstruct the so-called empirical knowledge that we have acquired through the course of our academic and non-academic life, while collectively constructing new ones, which should always be in the making. Just as it empowers us, knowledge can enslave us if we don't properly use it to effect individual and social changes. As we are vertiginously immersed in a technologically globalized world, which sometimes bombards us with massive misinformation, we need to develop a critical mind to dissect and deconstruct this massive misinformation so that we do not end becoming additional ideological agents who reproduce it and spread it in our schools, community, families, and in the larger world.

As I am writing the conclusion of this book, massive misinformation about the western and the restern world is being circulated through the media, then through our schools, families, and work places. Many of us as teachers and parents might feel overwhelmed by all this information and therefore do not know what to do. Consequently, we might decide to wait for our elected officials and policy makers to tell us what part of the information we should believe and what part of it we are allowed to share in school with our students, who invest their trust in us. We might naively believe what these elected officials and policy makers tell us, instead of questioning whether or not they are telling us the truth. This is the danger I hope that I would help readers of this book avoid by challenging them to question and analyze massive information, current issues that concern them or should concern them, and seek forbidden truths to which they have not been allowed to have access.

As I was finishing the manuscript of this book, in Latin America, leftist democratically elected leaders, such as Hugo Chávez in Venezuela, Evo Morales in Bolivia, and, more recently, Rafael Correa in Ecuador, and Daniel Ortega in Nicaragua, have been standing in firm opposition to U.S. neoliberal economic and political agenda. In Haiti, two years before Rene Preval got reelected as president in 2006, an elected president, Jean Bertrand Aristid, who stood firmly against the United States' neoliberal political and economic policies, was once more overthrown by a group of former soldiers supported by the US, Canada, and France. Immediately after Aristid was forced to leave power, foreign military forces were sent to Haiti and have been occupying it since. These military forces were led by the United Nations, whose goal was to "restore peace and order" there. However, despite their presence in this island, thousands of innocent people, especially women, have been raped and murdered. In fact, the soldiers of the United Nations have been accused of killing innocent Haitians in impoverished areas such as Cite Soleil (Sun city).

In an interview on December 29, 2006 with Amy Goodman, the hostess of Democracy Now! (an alternative TV/Radio show), a Haitian Human Rights activist, Lovinsky Pierre-Antoine, stated that:

What happened in Haiti is a continuation of a war of genocide against the poor population. In fact, that is an expression of the class struggle in Haiti. What happens is that the United Nations by what is called the MINUSTAH (United Nations Stabilization Mission in Haiti) is an accomplice of this war against the poor in Haiti.

In response to Mr. Pierre Antoine's testimony about the killing of poor Haitian people that took place in Cite Soleil, Juan Gonzalez, one of the journalists who was interviewing him, said:

I'd like to ask, in all my years as a journalist in terms of seeing how the United Nations operates in peacekeeping missions, I've never seen such periodic reports of the UN troops involved in aggressive, violent actions against populations as there has been in Haiti over the last few years. Do you [have] any sense of, on your part, why the UN is playing such a role in Haiti so different from what it's done around the world?

Similarly in Sudan, particularly in Darfur, and in Liberia it has been reported by Democracy Now! that young girls are being raped by soldiers, including UN soldiers.

While in the midst of writing this manuscript the United States invaded and occupied Afghanistan and Iraq. Since the U.S. invasion and occupation of these countries, innocent Iraqi children and elderly women have been killed, while journalists, peaceful activists and contractors have been kidnapped and killed as well.

While the U.S. was spending billions of dollars on the wars in Iraq and Afghanistan, New Orleans was destroyed by a horrible hurricane, Katrina. People, especially African American, poor white, elderly women, and children were displaced, and many of them did not survive the hurricane. All school buildings were destroyed and poor children spent months without being able to return to school. The U.S. government was indifferent to the plight of the poor and people with disabilities who did not receive adequate support before, during, and after the Hurricane so they could survive and recover from it.

Why do I deem it relevant and necessary to include some of the current world political and economic events in the conclusion of this book? One of many reasons is that I believe all systems of oppression, such as colonialism, racism, neocolonialism, and neoliberalism, as analyzed in this book, are intertwined. Therefore, to have a sound understanding of how these systems of oppressions operate and negatively impact humankind, it is imperative that they not only be linked to one another but also be contextualized.

With the rise of western neoliberal political and economic agenda, these issues require more attention than ever before because they are underlying causes of the uneven relation between western imperial powers and the restern world. And as a writer who does not want to be merely in but rather to be actively engaged with the world, I feel that I have an intellectual responsibility to be mindful of these current issues because they have impacted and shaped my thinking, writing, and consequently the content of this book. Therefore, to do otherwise will be a disservice to my inner self, political conviction, consciousness, and unshakable determination to challenge western imperial and neocolonial powers. Disregarding these issues will undermine one of the main reasons why this book is written. I wrote this book with the intention of challenging people to make a conscious effort to question the web of lies and try to transcend the climate of fear created and promoted through the mass media by western imperial and neocolonial powers. Specifically, I aim to challenge them to refute those lies and attempt to overcome that fear so they feel empowered to talk about and more importantly to take action against the ruinous effects of western globalization on people, especially poor people in the restern world.

School and the media, as pointed out in this book, have been two major ideological instruments that imperial and neocolonial powers have used to instill fear in and control the mind of neocolonial subjects. However, like millions of neocolonial subjects who have developed critical consciousness out of their daily struggles, I steadfastly refuse to allow the powerful to control my mind. For it is my tool of resistance to speak against all forms of social, economic, cultural, sexual, and political injustice wherever they take place. And as long as my mind is functional, I will firmly stand with whomever is a victim of these forms of injustice.

As the reader may have already noticed, this book partially reflects my lived experience as a neocolonial subject who lived in a neocolonized land, Haiti, for about twenty years and who has been living in an imperial land, the United States, for over a decade. Therefore, some of what I articulated throughout this book is a vivid testimony of such a lived experience, situated within the political, economic, social, and historical parameters of these two countries. Needless to point out that what I have had experienced in both lands have tremendously impacted and shaped my thinking and made me become a more involved and conscious political being.

It is worth emphasizing here that this book was already mentally conceptualized over a decade ago; however, I simply did not yet possess the proper discourse to put it into words. Stated otherwise, I did not then acquire the critical discourse that could have enabled me to map out the negative effects of western neocolonialism and neoliberalism on the restern world. Therefore, I chose to wait for over a decade, even though my inner desire to do so was burning my human conscience. Had I written this book fifteen years ago, I probably would have ended up writing it with the voice of a colonial subject who thinks a la Francaise or a la Americaine, that is, with a colonized or neocolonized mind. Instead of questioning the western political and economic hegemonic dominations of the restern world, I would have perhaps unconsciously glorified the imperial world, which does not serve the interest of people of my nationality, racial, cultural, and social class backgrounds. I hope this book, which is a product of my lived experience, ideology, political conviction, and acquired knowledge will be helpful and beneficial to whoever reads it. In writing it, I have no idea where it will take my voice. My hope is that my voice throughout this book will find and join oppressed voices that have been fighting for social, educational, economic, political, and sexual justice.

NOTES

I am immensely grateful to have lived long enough to write this book because, like many young intellectuals and non-intellectuals of my generation who have been unfairly incarcerated and/or were killed for daring to take a stance against human oppression, I could have been unjustly jailed, murdered, or just disappeared. May the almighty continue to bless me with his/her unconditional love, protect, and give me the strength to continuously write against educational, socioeconomic, political, racial, and gender inequities that affect us and therefore should concern us all!

REFERENCES

Ahmad, E. (2000). *Confronting Empire*. Cambridge, MA: South End Press.

Anzaldua, G. (1990). How to tame a wild tongue. In: R. Ferguson, M. Gever, T. Minh-Ha, & C. West (Eds). *Out there: Marginalization and contemporary cultures* (pp. 24-44). Cambridge, MA: MIT Press.

Atkinson, P. (1990). *The ethnographic imagination: Textual constructions of reality*. New York: Routledge.

Auerbach, E. R. (1995). The politics of the ESL classroom: Issues of power in pedagogical choices, In Tollefson, J. W. (1995). *Power and inequality in language education* (pp. 1-188). Cambridge, MA: Cambridge University Press.

Bakhtin, M.M (1986). *The dialogic imagination*. Austin: University of Texas Press

Bartolome, L. (1994). Beyond the methods fetish, toward a humanizing pedagogy. *Harvard Educational Review*, 64(2). 229-252.

Bhabha, H. (1994). *The location of culture*. London: Routledge.

Bhabha, H.K. (1983). Difference, Discrimination, and the Discourse of Colonialism, in F. Barker, P. Hulme, M. Iversen and D. Loxley (Eds).

Bhabha, H. (1994). *The location of culture*. London: Routledge.

Besterman, T et al. (1968). *The complete works of Voltaire*. Toranto: University of Toranto Press.

Bloom, A. (1987). *The closing of the American mind*. New York: Simon & Schuster.

Bourdieu, P. (1999). Language and symbolic power. In Adam Jaworski & Nikolas Coupland (Eds.). *The discourse reader* (pp. 502-514). London: Routledge.

Britzman, D. (1991). *Practice makes practice: A critical study of learning to teach*. Albany: State University of New York Press.

Cabral, A. (1973). *Return to the source: Selected speeches by Amilcar Cabral*. New York: Monthly Review Press.

Canagarajah, AS. (1993). Critical ethnography of a Sri Lankan classroom: Ambiguities in student opposition to reproduction in ESOL. *TESOL Quarterly, 27*:601-626.

Cesaire, A. (2000). *Discourse on colonialism*. New York: Monthly Review Press.

Chomsky, N. (1992). *What Uncle Sam really wants*. Berkeley, CA: Odonian Press.

Chomsky, N. (1996). *The common good*. Berkeley, CA: Odomian Press.

Chomsky, N. (1994). *Secrets, lies and democracy*. Berkeley, CA:Odonian Press.

Chomsky, N. & Herman, Edward. (1979). *The Washington connection and restern fascism*. Boston, MA: South End Press.

Chomsky, N. (2002). *Understanding power: The indispensable Chomsky*. The New Press, New York.

Condorcet, M. (1955). *Sketch for a historical picture of the progress of the human mind*. New York: Noonday Press.

Cope, B., and Kalantzis, M. (1993). *The powers of literacy: A genre approach to teaching writing*. Pittsburg, PA: University of Pittsburg Press.

Crawford, J. (1991). *Bilingual education: History, politics, theory and practice* (2nd ed.) Los Angeles, CA: Bilingual Educational Services.

Cummins, J. (1988). *Empowering minority students*. Sacremento, CA: California Association for Bilingual Education.

Danticat, E. (1996). We are ugly, but we are here, In *The birth of Caribbean Civilization: A century of ideas about culture and identity, nation and society* (pp.288-291). Kingston, Jamaica: Ian Randle Publishers.

Dash, M. J. (1988). *Haiti and the United States: National stereotypes and the literary imagination*. London: Macmillan.

Davidson, B. (1969). *Africa in history*. New York: Macmillan.

Dei,S. G. & Kempf, A. (2006). *Anti-colonialism and education*. Sense Publishers: Rotterdam/Taipei.

Delpit, L. (1996). The silenced dialogue: Power and pedagogy in educating other people's children. *Harvard Educational Review*. 280-298.

REFERENCES

De Montilla, N. A. (1971). *Americanization in Puerto Rico and the Public-School System 1900-1930* .Rio Piedras: Editorial Edil.

Derida, J. (1976). *Of gramatology*. Baltimore: Johns Hopkins Press.

Dewey, J. (1997). *Democracy and education*. New York: The Free Press.

Dimitriads, G., & Kamberelis, G. (2005). *Qualitative inquiry: Approaches to language and literacy research*. Teachers College Press: New York.

Diop. A. C. (1991). *Civilization or barbarism: An authentic anthropology*. New York: Lawrence Hill Books.

Doyle, M. W. (1986). *Empires*. Ithaca: Cornell University Press

Dyson, E. M. (2004). *The Michael Eric Dyson reader*. New York: Basic Civitas Books.

Eliot, T. S. (1932). *Critical Essays*. London: Faber & Faber

Engels, F. (1884). *The origin of the family, private property, and the state*. New York: International Publishers.

Ewig, C. (1999). Strengths and limits of the NGO women's movement model: Shaping Nicaragua's democratic institutions", *Latin American Research Review, 34*(3).

Fairclough, N. (1997). *Critical discourse analysis: The critical study of language*. London and New York: Longman.

Fanon, F. (1963). *The wretched of the earth*. Grove Press, New York.

Fanon, F. (1967). *Black skin white masks*. New York: Grove Press.

Fanon, F. (1965). *A dying colonialism*. New York: Grove Press.

Federici, S. (2004). *Caliban and the witch*. Brooklyn, NY: Automedia.

Firmin, A. *The equality of human races*. Chicago, Illinois: University of Illinois Press.

Foucault, M. (1980). *Two lectures, power and knowledge: Selected writings and other interviews*. New York: Pantheon.

Foucault, M. (1995/1977). *Discipline and punish: The birth of the prison* (trans. Alan Sheridan). New York; Vintage Books.

Fowler, H.D. (1987). *The mathematics of Plato's academy*. Oxford: Clarendon Press.

Freire,P. (1970). *Pedagogy of the oppressed*. New York: Seabury Press.

Freire,P. (1997). *Pedagogy of hope*. New York: Continuum Publishing Company.

Freire, P. & Macedo, D. (1987). *Reading the world and the word*. South Hadley, MA: Bergin and Garvey.

Galeano, E. (2000). *Upside down*. New York: Henry Holt and Company, LLC.

Gandhi, M.K. (1997). Hind Swaraj. In *Hind Swaraj and other writings*. Cambridge: Pearl.

Gardiner, M. (1992). *The dialogics of critique: M.M. Bakhtin and the theory of ideology*. London: Routledge.

Giroux, H. (1988). Border pedagogy in the Age of Postmodernism. *Journal of Education, 170*: 162-81.

Giroux, H & McLaren, P. (1994). *Between borders: Pedagogy and the politics of cultural studies*. New York: Routledge.

Gramsci, A. (1971). *Selections from the prison notebooks*. New York: International Publishers.

Haley, A. (1977). *Roots*. London: Pan Books

Hemming, J. (1970). *The conquest of the Incas*. New York: Hardcourt Brace and Company.

Hirsch, E.D., Jr. (1987). *Cultural literacy: What every American needs to know*. New York: Vintage.

Hogben, I. *Mathematics for the million*. London: Allen & Unwin.

Joseph, G. G. (1991). *The crest of the peacok: Now-European roots of mathematiques*. London: Penguin Books.

hooks, b.(1994). *Teaching to transgress: Education as the practice of freedom*. New York: Routledge.

Hughes, L. (1999). *Selected poems of Langston Hughes*. New York: Knopf.

Hume, D. (1902)). *Enquiries concerning the human understanding and concerning the principles of morals*. Oxford: Clarendon Press.

Luke, A. (1996). *Text and discourse in education: An introduction to critical discourse analysis*. New York: Routledge

Huston, Perdita. (1979). *Restern women speak out*. New York:

Routlege.

Kamat, S. (2000). Globalization/Paradox: Education, culture and the state in India. *Comparative Education Review, 40*(2).

Kemph, A. & Dei, S. (2006). Anti-colonial histororiography: Interrogating colonial education. In In Sefa, G.J. & Kempf (Eds), *Anti-colonialism and Education: The politics of resistance*. Rotterdam/Taipei: Sense Publishers.

Kerr, L. (2006). Engendering indigenous knowledge. In Sefa, G.J. & Kempf, A. (Eds), *Anti-colonialism and education: The politics of resistance* (pp.293-308). Rotterdam/Taipei: SensePublishers.

Kincheloe, J.L. & Semali, L.M. (1999). *What is indigenous knowledge? Voices from the Academy*. New York: Falmer Press.

Kneller, F. G. (1964). *Introduction to the philosophy of education*. New York: John Wiley & Sons.

Kozol, J. (1991). *Savage inequalities: Children in America's schools*. New York: Crown.

Kozol, J. (1985). *Illiterate America*. New York: Anchor Press/Doubleday.

Labouret, H. (1962). *Africa before the white man*. New York: Walker and Co.

Latouche, S. (1996). *The westernization of the world*. Cambridge, MA: Polity Press.

Leistyna, P. (1999). *Presence of mind: Education and the politics of deception*. Oxford: Wesview Press.

Lenin, I. V. (1943). *State and revolution*. New York: International Publishers

Loewen, James W. (1995). *Lies my teacher told me: Everything your American textbook got wrong*. New York: The new Press.

Montesquieu, B. D.(1975). *The spirit of the laws*. New York: Hafner Press.

Macedo, D. (1994). *Literacies of power: What Americans are not allowed to know*. Boulder: Westview.

McLeod, J. (2001). *Beginning postcolonialism*. Manchester University Press.

Memmi, A. (1965). *The colonizer and the colonized*. Boston, MA: Beacon Press.

Manigat, M. (2006). Haitian Women Still Fighting for Equality, *MassBay Magazine, 1*.

Manjoo, R. (2005). South Africa's National Gender Machinery, In Murray and O'Sullivan, (Eds). *Acta Juridica*. 260-272.

Marx, K. & Engels, F. (1975). The German ideology, In *Collected works, vol. 5*. New York: Random House.

McLeod, J. (2001). *Beginning postcolonialism*. Manchester University Press.

Michel, G. (1996). *Charlemagne Peralte and the first American occupation of Haiti*. Kendall and Hunt Publishing, Co., Dubuque, IA.

Mohanty, C. (1986). Under Western Eyes, In *Feminism without borders: Decolonizing theory, practicing solidarity*.

Morales, E. (2006) Interview. *Times Magazine*, June 5, *167*(23)

Nieto, S. (1992) *Affirming diversity: The sociopolitical context of multicultural education*. New York: Longman.

Ngugi Wa Thiong'o (1986). *Decolonizing the mind: The politics of language in African literature*. London: James Currey.

Nkrumah, K. (1970). *Africa must unite*. New York: International Publishers.

Nyerere, Julius. (1968). *Ujamaa: Essays on socialism*. Dar es Salem, Oxford University Press.

Obama, B. (2004). *The audacity of hope*. Democratic National Convention Keynote Address. Boston Massachusetts: Fleet Center.

Ogbu, J. & Simons, H. (1998). Voluntary and involuntary minorities: A cultural-ecological theory of school performance with some implications for education. *Anthropology & Education Quarterly, 29*(2): 155-188.

Olsen, R. (2003). Movie: *Rabbits Proof Fence*

Parenti, M. (1995). *Against empire: A brilliant expose of the brutal realities of U.S. global domination*. San Francisco: City Lights Books.

Phillipson, R. (1992). *Linguistic imperialism*. Oxford: Oxford University Press.

Pierre-Antoine, L. (2006), Interview. *Democracy Now!*, December 29.

Pitts, L. (2007), *The Republican*, February 5, A7 vol# 3

Plato. (1992). *Republic*. Indianapolis: Hackett Publishing Company.

137

REFERENCES

Pratt, M.L. (1999). Arts of the contact zone. In D. Bartholome (Ed.), *Ways of reading: An anthology for writers*. Boston: St. Martin's (5th ed.).

Radhakrishnan, R. (2003). *Theory in uneven world*. Malden, Massachusetts: Blackwell Publishing.

Robertson, R. (1992). *Globalization: Social theory and global culture*. London: Sage.

Robertson, R. (1997) Social theory, cultural relativity and the problem of globality, in: A. King (Ed.) *Culture of Minesota, globalization and the world system*, Minneapolis, MN, University.

Rodney, W. (1972). *How Europe underdeveloped Africa*. Washington, D.C.: Howard University Press.

Rousseau, J.J. (1968). *The social contract*. New York: Penguin Books.

Rousseau, J.J. (1966). *Emile Ou de L'education*. Paris: Garnier-Flammarion.

Roy, A. (2001). *Power politics*. Cambridge, Massachusetts: South End Press.

Roy, A. (2003). *War talk*. Cambridge, Massachusetts: South End Press.

Roy, A. (2006) Interview. *Democracy Now!*, May 24.

Said, E. (2003). *Culture and resistance*. Cambridge, MA: South End Press.

Said, E. (1993). *Culture and imperialism*. New York: Vintage Books.

Said, E. *Orientalism*. New York: Vintage Books

Sankara, T. (1984). *Thomas Sankara speaks*. New York: Pathfinder Press.

Sartre, J.P. In "Memmi, A. (1965). *The colonizer and the colonized*. Boston, MA: Beacon Press.

Sleeter, C. E., & Grant, C.A. (1987). An analysis of multicultural education in the United States. *Harvard Educational Review*. 421-444.

Seidman, S. (1994). *Contested knowledge: Social theory in the postmodern era*. Malden, Massachusetts: Blackwell Publishers.

Spivak, G.C. (1988). Can the subaltern speak? In C. Nelson and L. Grossberg (Eds.), *Marxism and the interpretation of culture* (pp. 271-313), Basingstoke: Macmillan Education.

Silverblatt, I. (1980). The universe has turned inside out... There is no justice for us here: Andean women under Spanish rule. In Etienne and Leacock, (Eds.), *Women and colonization: Anthropological Perspectives* (pp. 149-185). Westport, CT: Bergin & Garvey.

Spring, J. (2004). *Deculturalization and the struggle for equality*. New York: McGraw-Hill.

Stoler, A. Laura. (2002). *Carnal knowledge and imperial power: Race and the intimate colonial rule*. Los Angeles: University of California Berkeley.

Stiglitz, J. (2003). *Globalization and its discontents*. New York: W.W. Norton & Company.

Takaki, R. (1993). *A different mirror: A history of multicultural America*. New York: Little Brown and Company.

Teresi, D. (2002). *Lost discoveries: The ancient roots of modern science-from the Babylonians to the Maya*. New York: Simon & Schuster.

Villegas, A.M. (1988). School failure and cultural mismatch: Another view. *The Urban Review, 20* (4). 253-263.

Vygotsky, L. (1978). *Mind in society*. Cambridge, MA: Harvard University Press.

Wane, N.N. Is decolonization possible? In Sefa, G.J. & Kempf, A. (2006). *Anti-colonialism and education: The politics of resistance* (pp. 87-106). Rotterdam/Taipei: Sense Publishers.

Weinberg, S. (1992). *Dreams of a final theory*. New York: Pantheon Books.

Willet, J., Solsken, J., & Wilson-Keenan, J.-A. (1998). The (im) possibilities of constructing multicultural language practices in research and pedagogy. *Linguistics and Education, 10* (2), 165-218.

Young, J.C. R (2001). *Postcolonialism: A historical introduction*. Malden, MA: Blackwell Publishing.

Zinn, H. (2003). *A people's history of the United States*. New York: Harper & Row.

Zou, Y & Trueba, T. E. (1998). *Ethnic identity and power: Cultural contexts of political action in school and society*. State University of New York Press.

TRANSGRESSIONS: CULTURAL STUDIES AND EDUCATION

Cultural studies provides an analytical toolbox for both making sense of educational practice and extending the insights of educational professionals into their labors. In this context *Transgressions: Cultural Studies and Education* provides a collection of books in the domain that specify this assertion. Crafted for an audience of teachers, teacher educators, scholars and students of cultural studies and others interested in cultural studies and pedagogy, the series documents both the possibilities of and the controversies surrounding the intersection of cultural studies and education. The editors and the authors of this series do not assume that the interaction of cultural studies and education devalues other types of knowledge and analytical forms. Rather the intersection of these knowledge disciplines offers a rejuvenating, optimistic, and positive perspective on education and educational institutions. Some might describe its contribution as democratic, emancipatory, and transformative. The editors and authors maintain that cultural studies helps free educators from sterile, monolithic analyses that have for too long undermined efforts to think of educational practices by providing other words, new languages, and fresh metaphors. Operating in an interdisciplinary cosmos, Transgressions: Cultural Studies and Education is dedicated to exploring the ways cultural studies enhances the study and practice of education. With this in mind the series focuses in a non-exclusive way on popular culture as well as other dimensions of cultural studies including social theory, social justice and positionality, cultural dimensions of technological innovation, new media and media literacy, new forms of oppression emerging in an electronic hyperreality, and postcolonial global concerns. With these concerns in mind cultural studies scholars often argue that the realm of popular culture is the most powerful educational force in contemporary culture. Indeed, in the twenty-first century this pedagogical dynamic is sweeping through the entire world. Educators, they believe, must understand these emerging realities in order to gain an important voice in the pedagogical conversation.

Without an understanding of cultural pedagogy's (education that takes place outside of formal schooling) role in the shaping of individual identity—youth identity in particular—the role educators play in the lives of their students will continue to fade. Why do so many of our students feel that life is incomprehensible and devoid of meaning? What does it mean, teachers wonder, when young people are unable to describe their moods, their affective affiliation to the society around them. Meanings provided young people by mainstream institutions often do little to help them deal with their affective complexity, their difficulty negotiating the rift between meaning and affect. School knowledge and educational expectations seem as anachronistic as a ditto machine, not that learning ways of rational thought and making sense of the world are unimportant.

But school knowledge and educational expectations often have little to offer students about making sense of the way they feel, the way their affective lives are shaped. In no way do we argue that analysis of the production of youth in an electronic mediated world demands some "touchy-feely" educational superficiality. What is needed in this context is a rigorous analysis of the interrelationship between pedagogy, popular culture, meaning making, and youth subjectivity. In an era marked by youth depression, violence, and suicide such insights become extremely important, even life saving. Pessimism about the future is the common sense of many contemporary youth with its concomitant feeling that no one can make a difference.

If affective production can be shaped to reflect these perspectives, then it can be reshaped to lay the groundwork for optimism, passionate commitment, and transformative educational and political activity. In these ways cultural studies adds a dimension to the work of education unfilled by any other sub-discipline. This is what Transgressions: Cultural Studies and Education seeks to produce—literature on these issues that makes a difference. It seeks to publish studies that help those who work with young people, those individuals involved in the disciplines that study children and youth, and young people themselves improve their lives in these bizarre times.

OTHER BOOKS BY SENSE

ANTI-COLONIALISM AND EDUCATION
The Politics of Resistance Bottom of Form

George J. Sefa Dei and Arlo Kempf
Ontario Institute for Studies in Education,
University of Toronto

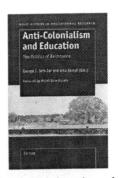

There is a rich intellectual history to the development of anti-colonial thought and practice. In discussing the politics of knowledge production, this collection borrows from and builds upon this intellectual traditional to offer understandings of the macro-political processes and structures of education delivery (e.g., social organization of knowledge, culture, pedagogy and resistant politics). The contributors raise key issues regarding the contestation of knowledge, as well as the role of cultural and social values in understanding the way power shapes everyday relations of politics and subjectivity. In reframing anti-colonial thought and practice, this book reclaims the power of critical, oppositional discourse and theory for educational transformation. The book also includes some the most current theorizing around anti-colonial practice. It is relevant for students, teachers, community/social workers and field practitioners interested in pursuit of education for social transformation. It is a must read for students of sociology, sociology of education, anthropology, political science and history.

BOLD VISIONS IN EDUCATIONAL RESEARCH Volume 7
ISBN 978-90-77874-55-4 hardback
ISBN 978-90-77874-18-9 paperback
326 pages

THE GREAT WHITE NORTH?
Exploring Whiteness, Privilege and Identity in Education

Paul R. Carr
Youngstown State University, USA

Darren E. Lund (Eds.)
University of Calgary, Canada

This landmark book represents the first text to pay critical and sustained attention to Whiteness in Canada from an impressive line-up of leading scholars and activists. The burgeoning scholarship on Whiteness will benefit richly from this book's timely inclusion of the insights of Canadian scholars, educators, activists and others working for social justice within and through the educational system, with implications far beyond national borders.

> Naming Whiteness and White identity is a political project as much as an intellectual engagement, and the co-editors of this collection must be commended for creating the space for such naming to take place in public and academic discourses. Is it noteworthy to acknowledge that both Paul and Darren are White, and that they are overseeing this work on Whiteness? I believe that it is, not because others cannot write about the subject with clarity and insight, as is clearly evident in the diverse range of contributors to this book. Rather, naming their positions as White allies embracing a rigorous conceptual and analytical discourse in the social justice field is an important signal that White society must also become intertwined in the entrenched racism that infuses every aspect of our society. As Paul and Darren correctly point out, race is still a pivotal concern for everything that happens in society, and especially in schools.

Excerpt from the Foreword by **George J. Sefa Dei** Professor and Chair, Department of Sociology and Equity Studies, Ontario Institute for Studies in Education of the University of Toronto (OISE/UT)

> The Great White North? provides a timely and important mode of addressing and examining the contradictions of Whiteness, and also challenging its insinuation into the very pores of the Canadian social universe. While the context of the book is distinctly Canadian, there are urgent messages here on race and anti-racism for the international community. Carr and Lund have provided educators with a vibrant contribution to the critical anti-racist literature. This is a book that needs to be put on reading- lists across the disciplines!

Peter McLaren
Professor, Graduate School of Education and Information Studies
University of California at Los Angeles

TRANSGRESSIONS: CULTURAL STUDIES AND EDUCATION Volume 11
ISBN 978-90-8790-142-4 hardback
ISBN 978-90-8790-143-1 paperback
264 pages

Printed in the United States
97036LV00001B/27/A